HOW TO WIN AND KE
TELLING THE TRUTH ABOUT YOUR BRAND

THE POWER OF PROMISE

KEN MOSESIAN

The Power of Promise. How to win and keep customers by telling the truth about your brand

Copyright © 2018 Ken Mosesian.

Book Design: Matías Baldanza, for Chasing Kites Publishing.

ISBN (paperback):   978-1-7327895-0-0

For a free audio copy, please visit Mosesian.com/promise

THE POWER OF PROMISE

How to win and keep customers by
telling the truth about your brand

By Ken Mosesian

"A story is a way to say something that can't be said any other way, and it takes every word in the story to say what the meaning is. You tell a story because a statement would be inadequate."

—Flannery O'Conner, quoted in *Life is a Verb*, by Patti Digh, p. xi

GET THE FREE AUDIO COPY OF THIS BOOK AT:

Mosesian.com/promise

CONTENTS

DEDICATION

To my mom, Lillian, who created a beautiful, welcoming home for our family. You understood your brand without ever knowing the term. You embodied hospitality. Whenever we had guests, planned or unplanned, you intuitively served plates of food and glasses of wine without ever asking if anyone was hungry or thirsty. *"You are all welcome here,"* you would announce. And indeed, they were. You left us far too early, but you live on in our hearts forever. Thank you, Mom. We love you.

To my husband, Bob. Thank you for agreeing to have an adventure with me 25 years ago. You make every day richer and there is no one else that I'd rather have as my companion on this journey. You approach life from the most exquisite place – that it will all work out in the end and that we should celebrate every day fully and completely. Thank you for helping me to realize that every moment is a gift. I love you.

To my dad, Wil, and my sister, Susan. Dad, you taught me that age is just a number. You should know. At 93-years young, you're volunteering five days a week at the police department, working out regularly, singing in choir, and teaching Sunday School. Susan, you protected, nurtured, and raised two beautiful children. You've run marathons, cycled centuries, climbed Mount Whitney, and climbed Kala Patthar on Mount Everest. And you continue to defy stereotypes of age every day with your extraordinary physical abilities. I love you and am in awe of you both.

INTRODUCTION

As I opened the kitchen door from the garage, the smell of Khouresh—an Assyrian beef stew—filled the air. I rounded the corner and there was my mom, standing over pots and pans on the stove, tending to the rice pilaf in the oven. My mouth started watering. I walked over, gave my mom a kiss, and turned to face the four men standing behind me.

"Mom, meet the Army paratrooper team. Team, meet my mom."

My dad, sister, and I had just returned from Castle Air Force Base where there was a twice-yearly air show. My sister thought these soldiers deserved a home-cooked meal, which of course they did.

This would have freaked most moms out. Given our ethnic background though (Armenian and Assyrian, and as I recently discovered through Ancestry.com, Italian and Greek), there was always plenty of food. *"Portions"* did not exist in our home. Pots, kettles, roasters—those were the ways we measured quantities of food. For my mom, four extra mouths for dinner was a walk in the park.

3

The guys all greeted my mom, and without missing a beat, she said, *"Now I'm feeding them from the sky. Boys, the bathroom is straight ahead. Wash up and have a glass of wine. Dinner is in an hour."*

Laughter and conversation flowed as everyone relaxed into being part of our family for the night. As we sat down for dinner, my mom stood up, raised a glass, looked around the table at these former strangers who were now guests in our home, and said, *"You are all welcome here."*

That experience was over thirty years ago, and I remember it like it was yesterday. Something clicked for me in that moment. Hospitality. Treating the stranger like a friend. Welcoming those previously unknown into your home. Unconditional acceptance. Sharing food and drink. Loving people you have never met. These were the hallmark attributes of my mom's life, the qualities that people could count on when spending time with her.

Looking back, I remember that every detail was attended to and that those soldiers were shown the same kindness that we would have shown to family members. Not just because they were soldiers, but because they were guests in our home.

Extraordinary hospitality was mom's personal brand. Her promise. And she delivered the promise of her brand every time. Anyone that walked through our doors, or in this case, dropped in from the skies, was welcome. There would be wine and food and always more than enough. There was a reason we had three refrigerators and a full-size deep freeze: never would anyone be told *"we're out of food."*

"You are all welcome here."

***

Ten years later, after her second bout with cancer, we lost my mom to that horrific disease. We had the intense experience of having her home on hospice care during her last few weeks. My sister and I did everything we could to provide my mom with the same hospitality she had shown countless others throughout her life. Escorting my mom on her final journey on earth was the best and worst experience of my life.

We set her bed up in the family room in front of the fireplace. My spouse brought in her favorite flowers—lilies—and attended to them daily. My mom wanted to receive guests and didn't have a bed jacket (a short upper garment worn over a nightgown). Again, my husband came to the rescue with a few well-placed calls to Bloomingdale's, and my mom had what she wanted to properly greet those coming to say goodbye.

Wednesday afternoon, as I was playing her favorite hymns on the piano in the living room, my sister came in and said that mom had asked if it was OK to close her eyes and not open them again.

"What should I tell her?" Susan asked me.

I replied, *"Tell mom, yes. It is OK."*

About forty-five minutes later, my sister came back into the living room, laughing. I thought my mom was gone and that Susan was having a slightly hysterical reaction.

It turns out that my mom had just opened her eyes, looked around, and said, *"Am I still here?"* We all had a good laugh, shared a popsicle or two, and prepared ourselves for what we knew was the inevitable.

Caring for someone who is dying is a detailed business, and my sister and I made a great team naturally taking on different, complementary responsibilities both during mom's hospitalization and during her home hospice care. There was an intricate list to carry out: tracking doses of morphine, making sure her pain was being managed, keeping her nourished and hydrated, communicating with her, listening to her, and then having the most difficult conversations ever—the ones about the funeral, which signaled that we all officially accepted this was coming to an end. There was also the making of promises—no open casket (except for one hour, unannounced, and only open to family), the dress that she would be buried in, and her favorite hymns to be sung. Details matter.

The evening that my mom died she waited (and I use the term deliberately) until we were just out of the family room and in the kitchen. She had always cautioned us to not hover and stare, and I think she wanted to slip away as unobtrusively as possible, which she did.

In the ensuing hours, my Type AAA personality kicked into high gear. I made a master task list, created a three-ring binder with tabs, and assigned responsibilities. We started making calls.

The mortuary attendants arrived, and we said the most surreal goodbye as our mom's body was zipped into a black bag. We kept moving because there was a new focus. We had two services to plan and prepare for—Evensong (sung evening prayer) at the funeral home and the funeral at the church the next day.

Musicians had to be booked and flown in. Music needed to be procured and copied. The last photo of her from a few weeks before at Christmas needed to be enlarged and framed so it could stand by her casket. And I was determined to keep my word to my mom with every detail.

The hymns she loved would be sung, and she would be buried in the clothes she requested. We would have a full Assyrian dinner afterwards, and it would feature the same foods that we had the night the paratrooper team floated in. Because in our culture, whether you're celebrating or mourning, the table reigns supreme.

We went casket shopping and settled on something we thought was perfect. We confirmed the plot at the cemetery, the time of the arrival, and I made sure I had contact names and numbers in case of emergencies.

I met with the pastor to review the order of the service. My husband and his sister created a casket cover by hand that featured about 1,000 lemon leaves glued in a circular pattern, and attached 33 gardenias to it (another one of my mom's favorite flowers) re-calling the 33 years that Jesus lived on earth. Given the depth of her faith, I knew how much this detail would mean to her.

On the day of the first service at the funeral home, we stopped by in the afternoon as the flowers were being delivered. My husband, staring in horror at the way some of the arrangements were put together, turned to the funeral director and said, *"I need a bucket with water, a roll of paper towels, sharp scissors, and a garbage can."*

Over the next couple of hours, he literally created an entire new set of floral arrangements, transforming the raw materials into things of beauty. We took a short break to change, and then it was time for the first service.

There is something otherworldly about saying goodbye to your mom, particularly at a younger age. You keep thinking that she'll appear at dinner or that she'll pick up the phone if you call her. Because that's the way it's always been, and to have it end, forever, is incomprehensible.

I walked away from it knowing that the planning, the details, the caring, the compassion, the desire to create an extraordinary and unforgettable experience for everyone who knew and loved my mom was worth the three sleepless days and nights for my sister and me. It was worth it a hundred times over.

I knew it in my heart. I knew it when the director of the funeral home said that she had never seen a service carried out with such grace and dignity in her thirty years in the business. I knew it when my dad simply said, *"Thank you."*

✳✳✳

Looking back on that chapter of my life, I understand why I am where I am today, and why I love doing what I do. That's why I approach business from the perspective of relationship.

By her example, my mom taught me about personal integrity, making and keeping promises, and creating experiences that bring joy to people and make them feel like they matter. Those are the kinds of experiences that will turn your one-time purchasers into repeat customers and brand advocates for your business.

The promise of this book is that the simple act of making a promise and keeping it—relentlessly and in every aspect of your company—will radically shift the success of your business for the better.

Studies vary, but as discussed in a Harvard Business Review article, acquiring a new customer is 5 to 25 times more expensive than retaining a current one. Research done by Bain & Company cited in the same Harvard Business review article demonstrates that increasing retention rates by five percent increases profits by 25 to 95 percent (Gallo, 2014).

The Power of Promise will help you not only win, but also retain as many customers as possible, converting them into brand advocates for your company.

The deeper, and perhaps more meaningful, promise is that by integrating this work into all aspects of your life, beginning with yourself and including your relationship with your family and friends, will lead to a more satisfying human experience, which will also be good for business, because people are attracted to authenticity.

BRAND IS EMOTIONAL AND EXPERIENTIAL

"Don't be so emotional—this is business." You've most likely heard a variation on this theme at some point. Business is about numbers. Numbers are emotionless. True enough, but if you want to see those numbers move in the right direction, then you need to care about how your customers feel in relation to the product or service you provide to them. Even though numbers are emotionless, people are not, particularly when it comes to promises kept and promises broken.

This is demonstrated in a 2018 survey conducted by PricewaterhouseCoopers (PwC), where one third of all global consumers said they would leave a brand they loved after one bad experience. The same study found that the top three things that would stop customers from doing business with a brand are lack of trust in the company, unfriendly service, and bad employee attitude—all qualities of relationships (Clarke and Kinghorn, 2018).

That's why it is critical to understand what promise your brand is making to your customers and to declare it. Then you can map the ideal customer journey, train your teams, and deliver the promise of your brand through outstanding experiences to everyone who interacts with your company.

This is the biggest challenge—and opportunity—facing your company today: **knowing your brand promise and consistently delivering it.**

Every time someone *"touches"* your brand, they're measuring you against the expectations they have formed in a myriad of ways: seeing an ad, visiting your website, following your social media feeds, reading reviews, talking with others, walking into your store, calling you on the phone. They are testing your brand in real time to see if it aligns with your promise. If it does, your brand is enhanced. If it does not, your brand is degraded. There is no neutral.

Your customer may not even realize that every experience with your brand is a test, but it is. Every day is Judgment Day. Does your product or service live up to the promise that you said it would? To put it bluntly, are you telling the truth or are you lying?

Harsh, I know. But that's the underlying truth, and everyone understands that the opposite of the truth is a lie, and no one wants to do business with a liar.

The Power of Promise is my commitment to guide you through five key steps:

- UNDERSTAND brand and customer experience
- DECLARE your own brand
- MAP the ideal customer experience
- TRAIN your team
- DELIVER the promise of your brand internally and externally

A video with practical tips about the Five Key Steps and exercises your team can use is available at: <u>Mosesian.com/promise</u>

Integrity, and all it implies—honesty, trustworthiness, wholeness—will be our guide and our goal: integrity with customers, prospects, employees, friends, family, and most importantly, with yourself. You are the foundation on which everything else is built.

Over the past two decades, I've worked with a diverse array of businesses in the profit and nonprofit worlds, helping them to understand that their brand is their promise to the customer and that their brand is also personal and emotional.

In the process of doing this work with my clients, something extraordinary happens. Employees report a sense of ease as the experiences that they provide their customers align with the promise of the company's brand. Customer satisfaction increases and previously dissatisfied customers regain trust in the brand. Why? *Integrity*.

Three brief stories illustrate how customers felt lied to when the promise of the brand was not delivered. You'll notice that if you changed some of the details, you might think that we're talking about a relationship with a boyfriend or girlfriend gone bad.

As you read, you'll quickly realize that these *are* relationships, and relationships live or die based on trust. In each case, a promise was made and not kept. Trust was breached.

***

Example #1: I'll take my embryos to go.

A woman struggling with infertility was increasingly dismayed by the service she was receiving at her physician's office. This particular fertility doctor had been first to market in the area, and as other practices moved in, this doctor's company seemed to take for granted that their patients would continue to come to them, no matter the quality of their service.

Over time, their promise of compassionate care had become empty. One day, after more than a year of struggling to conceive, and perceiving that her business was indeed being taken for granted, she decided to take the future of her family into her own hands.

Literally.

She showed up in the waiting room during a peak morning hour and demanded her frozen embryos. She announced that she had done some *"comparison shopping,"* and was heading to a competing practice. The waiting room fell silent as the front desk went into panic mode.

After the incident, one of the physicians told me that he never imagined that his patients would actually *"kick the tires"* of other practices. Yet that's exactly what she did. And she let the world know about it. Social media, anyone?

***

Example #2: Home away from home becomes hotel away from home.

A seasoned business traveler had always counted on a particular international hotel to be his home away from home. That's how they advertised themselves. That was the promise of their brand. For five years they had always delivered, and it meant a lot to him.

This business traveler left a young family behind each time he boarded the plane, but he was working for financial independence by age forty-five, and the early sacrifice felt like it would be worth the payoff. The hotel knew his story and did everything they could to make him feel at home.

Over the course of his regular and frequent stays, the concierge got to know him and what he missed about being at home. He missed a favorite scented candle that his wife would always have burning in the bathroom saying it made the place feel like a spa. The concierge made sure to purchase several, and from that day on there was one burning in his bathroom every time he arrived. They got to know his birthday, anniversary, the names of his wife and children, and would often have small, unique gifts for them that he could take back home. In short, they delivered the promise of their brand. The hotel became his home away from home, and the staff became part of his extended family. Just like the advertisement promised.

Then management changed hands, and along with it, the staff. The hotel kept advertising the *"home away from home"* brand but didn't bother to compare their view of the brand to that of the previous management.

For the new managers, home away from home meant a clean room, comfy chairs, sofas with pillows, and a great bed. It meant a bathroom fully stocked with every amenity. Though the new staff was friendly, the quality of being part of the family disappeared without a trace, as this was not how the new managers envisioned a home-away-from-home hotel.

If the new staff had gotten to know this client and treated him the same way he had been accustomed to, he would have gladly remained a loyal customer. But they didn't, and in spite of the excellent service, he felt like a stranger. He began staying at another hotel.

***

Example #3: Missing the mark at 30,000 feet.

A couple had been saving for two years to take their honeymoon, which would also be their first trip to Europe. They scoured the websites for multiple airlines, comparing business class services. Round trip tickets to Europe were going to cost them about $10,000 for two. For this couple, $10,000 was a big deal. They wanted to get it right and they thought they had.

I spoke to them after they returned home, and they explained that they had a fantastic time, which was followed by a long pause. After a bit of coaxing, they shared that the business class experience (while infinitely better then flying economy) didn't live up to the photos, the narrative on the website, and the expectations they had formed in their minds, which caused them to fall in love with this brand before even using their product.

Yes, they had flatbed seats. Yes, they had a good food and wine selection. Yes, they were expedited through security. But the plane was a bit shabby inside. The tray tables looked like they hadn't been wiped down. The flight attendants were professional, but

14

not particularly friendly, even after sharing that this was their honeymoon, their first trip in business class, and their first trip to Europe. The features were there, but the promised experience that the website alluded to—class, elegance, style—never materialized, and they felt let down.

For this couple, there would never be another honeymoon, another first trip to Europe, another first experience in business class. The journey was so much of the honeymoon for these travelers that they talked more about what the flight would be like more than they talked about the sights they would see while in Europe. The airline had one shot, and they failed. This couple became a statistic, part of the one-third of consumers who walked away from a brand they loved after one bad experience.

IT BEGINS WITH YOU

If you take to heart and put into practice the advice that follows, you will see tangible improvement in your business. Paying attention to everything that this book delves into—from knowing your brand to leadership and communication skills and effectively evaluating your customers' experiences—can only enhance your bottom line. It will also make the working experience of your staff measurably better.

Back in the day, I took a course called the Landmark Forum. At the outset, our instructor said that we could take the $199 course, or the million-dollar course, and they both cost $199. She went on to explain that by simply showing up and being present in the room we would get something out of it. But by showing up fully, participating in everything 100%, and then executing what we learned in all aspects of our lives, we would be engaging the million-dollar course.

I really liked the idea of getting a million-dollar value for $199! And, I wanted to put the promise of the course to the test. So I dove straight into the deep end. The results were stunning. Shortly after the course concluded, I got a new job, began my consulting work, found the love of my life (whom I'm still with twenty-five years later), began enjoying a new confidence in myself and my decisions, and created a more powerful relationship with my parents.

The Landmark Forum was a set of tools, a catalyst for change that helped me gain access to who I really am. By stripping away the stories about who I said I was and then connecting to who I really am, all resistance to fulfilling my dreams fell away. Suddenly, I went from pursuing things to attracting everything that I desired at that time in my life: my perfect spouse, a great relationship with my parents, a new career, loving friends, and health and wellness.

So too it is with this work. We will explore insights into better communication, leadership, strategy, understanding your brand, and a myriad of other items that can only help your business improve. To use the already-cited example, you'll get value from this book. But as long as you're already investing time to read it, and hopefully putting into play the recommendations that I've made within its pages, why not step into million-dollar territory? And why not begin with you?

Simply stated, this means you'll need to take inventory of your own life. Because not only are customers testing your company's brand every time they interact with it, everyone with whom you interact is testing you and your personal brand, consciously and subconsciously. We are all, in a word, judges. All of us. We judge everything.

The challenge I issue is this: apply everything from this book that fits your business, and also apply it to yourself as well. The inventory begins with one question: How often do I keep my promises? To myself? To my family and friends? To my co-workers and customers?

As I'll say many times, your word is your bond. Anything that comes out of your mouth is a promise, whether or not you said *"I promise."* That's a game that a five-year-old plays.

The easiest way to begin is to keep a simple list of everything you promise. From a casual, personal promise of *"Yeah, I'll call you back"* to a formal, business promise of *"I'll make sure to credit your account for the refund,"* it all matters. Details matter.

Why bother?

Because this exercise, which I recommend you try on a daily basis for thirty days, will cause you to be mindful of what comes out of your mouth and whether or not you follow through.

Are you telling the truth, or are you lying?

Again, whether or not you construe what you say as a promise, if you give someone an assurance that something will happen, it's a promise. That has consequences. As I mentioned above, we're always judging. Even if the person to whom you said you would call back knows that you're not telling the truth, on some level, they also know you as a person who doesn't keep your word.

If we take the time to rigorously examine everything that we promise in writing or in conversation, and then hold ourselves accountable to keeping it, the perception of who we are changes.

Others see us differently, and we begin to see ourselves differently too.

To be circumspect about what we say in personal matters is often times much more difficult than what we say in professional matters. For some reason, we seem to not care as much about our personal brand as we do our business. Or perhaps more accurately stated: we seem to think that *"white lies"* and *"half-truths"* will not have a significant impact on our personal brand.

Whether you are a business owner or an employee deeply invested in delivering on your organization's promise via its brand, the most powerful way to fulfill that promise begins with you being aligned with who you really are.

CHAPTER ONE
UNDERSTAND

BEING HUMAN, BRAND, AND CUSTOMER EXPERIENCE

In this chapter, we'll start at the VERY beginning, back to when we roamed the earth in tribes of about forty people. We'll look at why 30,000 years later we're still hardwired to believe the worst, fear rejection, and crave acceptance. Then we'll fast forward to the present day and clarify the key topics of discussion: brand promise and customer experience. We'll talk about WHY experiences matter and recommend some practical steps you can take to transfer this information from your head to your heart.

***

Silence. It felt worse than anything I had previously experienced in my thirteen years on earth. Absolute dead silence. I had given a note to the love of my life professing my undying passion for her as best as a seventh-grader could. I even taped a coin to the letter so she could use a phone booth for privacy when returning my call. (No, mobile phones did not exist when I was a kid.)

I was certain that the call would not only come, but that her declaration of love for me would be every bit as deep as mine for her, requiring that she make the call outside of her house so that we could at long last speak the truth to each other. Yes, it sounds like a really bad junior high school soap opera. But it felt deadly serious to me.

A week passed, and nothing. No communication whatsoever. Summer break was coming to an end, and I would have to face her at school in a few days. When I did finally see her, it was as if the note had never been given. Not a word was said about it. I didn't cry. I felt gutted. I thought I was going to die.

Why?

Survival. Deeply coded in our DNA, rejection still brings up near-death feelings in us, even when our life isn't in danger.

THE BIOLOGY OF BEING HUMAN

Survival.

In a word, that's what got us here, and that's what keeps us going. But the reality of life has changed radically from when we first formed into communities about 30,000 years ago.

Being a part of a community back then was essential to surviving life on earth. People learned early on that it was important to demonstrate value to the group, so as to remain in it.

Could you hunt and gather? Did you have the kind of strength that could be used to build shelters, haul wood, or fight off wild animals or rival tribes? Did you have a mind that could figure out how to keep everyone safe and warm during a horrific winter or outsmart a rival, warring tribe? Were you valued for your looks, and subsequently for your sexual prowess, because the community needed to continually replenish its members?

There could be no dead weight. Everyone had to bring something to the table, or risk rejection. And it's not as if one could simply join another community. Think of how sparsely populated the earth was. Tribes could wander for weeks and not come upon another tribe. You would be abandoned to face the elements and the animals alone. You would have to forage for your own food, provide for your own defense, and build your own shelter. The fact is though, if you possessed those skills, you wouldn't have been abandoned!

This abject fear of rejection and utter elation of acceptance was coded in our DNA long ago, and it still remains. Rejection equals death. Acceptance equals life.

Think about how we judge people: she's beautiful, he's strong, she's got a brilliant mind. Tens of thousands of years later, we still use the same criteria to judge the value of other human beings, at least at the outset. And we use those same criteria to project the version of ourselves that we want others to see. Think of how we curate our social media. We craft our *"shares"* based on perceived judgment, only posting the best of ourselves: vacations (preferably to exotic and/or expensive locations), working out at the gym (getting in progressively better shape), being accepted to the best school, celebrating a promotion, or dressing to the nines for that dinner of a lifetime.

We reinforce what matters and put it on full display. The stakes are different now in that we're not going to literally die if we're rejected by someone or by a group, but the encoded feelings haven't changed. Our survival DNA believes that things are just as dire as they once were. Hence, my reaction when my hoped-for girlfriend silently dumped me.

Think back to a time when someone broke up with you, or you didn't get accepted into the sorority or fraternity that you were pledging. Maybe you were rejected from the first college of your choice. Perhaps, like me, you were always picked last for the sports team. It was made clear that you added no perceptible value, and if the coach had not been there, you would have been left on the sidelines. How do these experiences of modern-day rejection leave us feeling? Crushed, more often than not. It's not uncommon to hear people say, *"I feel like I'm going to die"* or *"this is killing me."*

Survival. It still haunts us today.

That's not to say it's a bad thing. If we valued hugs and empathy more than strength, intelligence, and sex appeal back then, our human race probably would have only lasted one generation. It's also why we're more inclined to pay attention to fear-based news rather than positive news, and generally, to assume something negative will happen before we assume that something positive will occur. In the hierarchy of attention, fear is the clear leader, followed by sex, and then finally good news.

Why? Negative occurrences have the potential to kill us. Positive ones do not. We give our attention to that which we feel may affect our survival, whether it will or it won't. This is why negative campaign ads tend to be effective.

When given the choice between hearing negative or positive news, most of us will choose the negative news every time in order to protect ourselves from possible cataclysmic events (up to and including death). This choice is almost guaranteed because our survival response is far more powerful than our desire for pleasure.

Advertisers use this technique with great success. They create scarcity—*"Only three spaces left in the seminar!"* They create anxiety—*"Prices increase by 50 percent tonight at midnight, so act now!"* They create exclusivity—*"You must interview to apply to be accepted into the program!"*

These techniques play into our fear of rejection and our desire to be part of a group. They touch on other aspects of fear including the fear of missing out and the fear of looking like a fool.

Advertisers also create an inflated sense of value and spark the notion that there's a growing wave of support for this product or service. I mean, if there are only three seats left, it is obviously a popular program, and if it's popular, it must be worthwhile, and I certainly don't want to miss out on that!

Why are these things good to be aware of other than for some interesting cocktail hour conversation? Because people can focus more completely on positive things once the threats are removed. Even if the threat isn't a charging, wild animal, any perceived threat is just as distracting. If we can anticipate the negative concerns customers have and dispel them early on, we have a much better opportunity to be successful in creating meaningful and exceptional customer experiences.

This knowledge also serves as a warning: people are genetically programmed to be on alert so anything that feeds into the narrative of danger is going to detract from whatever amazing experiences you are creating for them.

Something as seemingly minor as a coffee stain on a seat back tray, or an online shopping cart that falters a moment too long during checkout, or a customer service representative who tells you there's no way to track your product: all of these are examples of customer experiences that can trigger a *"danger"* response.

The coffee stain example is worth examining further. A study demonstrated that customers construe a seemingly simple stain to mean that the airline doesn't properly maintain its aircraft, which translated to the airworthiness of the plane itself and then to the competency of the pilot. All because of a coffee stain on a tray table. Details matter.

It's also good to remember that we rely on our feelings for feedback. If something doesn't *"feel right,"* we tend to proceed with caution or not proceed at all. Likewise, and sometimes in direct contradiction to the facts, some things *"just feel right."*

We use this feedback mechanism most frequently when we confront situations that are new to us: a first meeting, a first date, the first time we walk into a new shop or visit a website, but even still it is always in action.

A final note about community: it matters. It always has and it always will. Now more than ever, human beings crave a sense of belonging. This is powerful information as you seek to serve your clients and customers. Think about how you're not only providing a superior experience to accompany your product or service, but how you're also creating a community in the process. There's value in people feeling like they are part of a group, especially one that has some sort of X factor associated with it. You get to design that. You get to infuse the X factor. You get to decide what kinds of feelings you want to evoke by bringing people together, using your product or service as the vehicle.

BRAND PROMISE

Why care about making a promise or about the kind of experience that a customer has? After all, it's a transaction, right? You provide a product or service. The customer pays for it. Done!

But it's not that simple. *Humans are experiential beings and collectors of experiences.* You're *not* just selling a computer, or an accounting service, or a sandwich. You're selling the totality of the experience, the emotion that goes with it, and the promise underlying it all.

As we'll explore in great detail, *everything* about your business contributes to the promise that you're making, both implicitly and explicitly, to your customers.

Everyone approaches your business (online or brick and mortar) with some sort of expectation even if they're visiting for the first time. Then, the moment they arrive and see, hear, smell, touch, or taste, additional impressions are instantly formed, ancient responses encoded in our DNA are activated, and emotions are triggered.

People may be reminded of a previous experience they had with your business and will bring that memory to bear on their current expectation. They may recall someone else's story about the experience they had with your business. Your store or site may trigger a thought about a competing business, which causes the customer to question how you will compare.

Even if there's not a conscious awareness of what's happening, all of these emotions occur in each of us, every moment of every day. We collect. We distill. We compare. We judge.

We judge.

That's the heart of the matter. We judge. Does the promise that was communicated match our experience? If it does, the brand is enhanced. If it doesn't, the brand is degraded. There is no neutral.

If the promise of the brand was kept, this experience will be one that we, as consumers, will want to replicate and share with others. If the promise of the brand was not fulfilled, this experience will be one that we will avoid repeating, which warns others to do the same.

All of this is to say that the power of promise is extraordinary. Most of us don't realize that we're actually giving our word that our product or service will deliver something.

We talk about creating campaigns, and reaching target markets, about market penetration and domination, but how often do we talk about making a promise to our prospects and customers and then keeping it? Again, let's be clear, it doesn't matter if you actually say, *"I promise."* That's the response of a five-year-old. You gave your word. Your word is your bond. Live by it.

A promise kept is restorative. It restores our faith in fellow human beings. It makes us feel good about ourselves and about the one who made and kept the promise. It gives us hope. You may think that these feelings increase with the value of the product or service, but they don't.

Remember, with brand we're not tapping into logic, but rather feelings. Primal feelings. Feelings which are not dependent on the type or cost of an item or a service, but feelings that are dependent on the customer's experience as an *extension* of the product or service.

Years ago, my spouse, Robert, and I were at the Burbank Airport heading to Sacramento for Christmas with our families. We carried with us a beautiful set of six steak knives we had purchased in Paris. The knives were boxed, wrapped, and neatly tucked inside our carry-on luggage.

As we went through security, we were pulled aside and asked if we had knives in our luggage. *"We do,"* we exclaimed and proceeded to tell the security agent that they were manufactured by the same company that made swords for Napoleon, and, in fact, had the same bee insignia on the top of the blade as his weapons did.

We even told him about this great shop in Paris where we purchased them and how excited we were to give them to our sister for Christmas. I remember telling him that we had a set ourselves at home, and they are as sharp as surgical steel.

The guy looked at us like we were high and said, *"They're knives."*

"Yes, just like we told you."

He explained that six surgically sharp steak knives were not allowed in the cabin, as they could be used as weapons, which upon reflection makes sense given that they were made by a weapons manufacturer.

My spouse replied, *"But they're wrapped! We would never tear the wrapping paper!"* To be fair, they really were beautifully wrapped in some pretty snazzy paper, and we never would have thought of ripping it off.

He was not moved, *"Go check them. Now!"*

We rushed back to the counter and told the agent what had happened. She was very sweet saying that she would never have touched the wrapping paper either, but rules being what they were she needed to check the knives for us.

The problem was that our bags were already on the plane. The kind agent asked for our claim tag numbers and a description of our bags. She promised us that she would personally take the knives out to the plane, locate one of the bags, place the knives in it, and give us a big *"thumbs up"* from the tarmac.

If you know Burbank, you know that the terminal is lined with windows at the tarmac level, and you can clearly see what's going on with each aircraft. We waited by the windows and watched her run out to the plane. In a couple of minutes, she emerged from the baggage hold, gave us the thumbs up, and we proceeded back to security. Once we retrieved our bags in Sacramento, we opened them up and found our knives safely tucked inside.

I called Southwest to commend the employee and wrote a letter to her supervisor as well. This was an experience that happened in 2000, and I'm still retelling it to this day. It made the kind of lasting impression that cannot be achieved by any other means. It was worth more than the very best advertising. And it illustrates so many points that relate to brand and customer experience.

Southwest's brand symbol is the heart. They consider humanity and a personal touch to be the mainstays of their culture. They empower their team members with flexibility in how they deal with various customer service challenges. They talk about *"LUV,"* and their pre-flight announcements are legendary. Three of their core values are having a Fun-LUVing Attitude, having a Servant's Heart, and providing *"Friendly Customer Service."* (A quick quiz: What are the top three reasons from the PwC study that causes customers to stop doing business with a brand? You got it! Bad employee attitude, unfriendly customer service, and not trusting the company. Years ago, without any survey, Southwest got it right.)

We experienced all of that and more. We were never made to feel anything other than valued. Remember that the counter agent told us she would never have opened wrapping paper that nice either. She went so far above and beyond as to run out to the plane herself, thereby taking personal responsibility for the delivery of our gift.

This is something that I refer to as 100% responsibility. In fact, if you would have told us that she was really one of the chief executives of the company or a major stockholder, we would have believed it.

But why? Why did this experience have such an impact? Because she approached our situation from the perspective of ownership. She knew that her company's reputation was on the line with every customer interaction. We had shared with her some of the details of the knives, what made them special, and why the person we were giving them to was going to love them, and she had listened with genuine interest and enthusiasm. She recognized that this was far more than just a set of knives. It was a heartfelt expression of love for one of our family members, and how she handled the situation reflected that she could see how important they were.

The Southwest agent clearly understood that brand is emotional and customer experience is relationship based, and it showed.

What if your business is web-based? The same basic principles apply.

We each know what it feels like to experience a website that makes us feel good. Site navigation is intuitive. The look and feel of the site inspires confidence, and you feel as though you're truly interacting with it and it with you. You get a sense of security, believing your information will be protected. You're not forced to create an account to make a purchase.

There are multiple ways to complete your purchase. There are options for international purchases and shipping. There are no surprise add-on charges at the very end of the process. The site performs well, and there are no hiccups or, heaven forbid, a crash, as you enter your credit card information.

Confirmation of your purchase with all the details is immediately provided, including ship date, estimated delivery date, tracking number, and an available help or chat line. You're kept updated when the product ships and when it arrives.

If you do need to contact customer support, you're given options to connect in the way that's most meaningful to you: email, chat, text, social, or phone. And when you do contact them, your problem is resolved in your favor and quickly.

That's a huge list, and obviously, there's much more going on in terms of actual programming and user experience design to create a seamless, *"feel good"* experience. The point is, it takes intentional thought and equally intentional follow through to create an experience that immediately moves people from their DNA fear and survival instincts to having the experience that will please them, and keep them coming back, whether in person or online.

Ultimately, people want to do business with brands that help them solve their problems and make them feel good. People that they like. People that they trust because they keep their promises. In the PwC study, 75 percent of US consumers name customer experience as an important factor in their purchasing decision, but only 49 percent say companies actually do provide a good customer experience.

In an American Express study, 7 out of 10 Americans were willing to spend more money with a company that provided excellent customer service (American Express, 2017). It's worth it. If you want to level up your service, think about what you're doing to add meaning to someone's life. Recall how my spouse added 33 gardenias to my mom's casket cover. That one seemingly small act left an indelible imprint of significance on our final goodbye. There are an infinite number of ways you can provide meaning, large or small.

A promise that is kept is worth more than any paid advertising can ever buy.

The power of promise applies to profit and non-profit businesses, communities of faith, and other non-profit organizations. In the case of the latter, the *"customer"* might be a church congregant or maybe a charitable donor, but the principles are the same.

In the for-profit world, money is given to receive a product or service. In a church or other non-profit organization, money is given to advance the mission.

Whatever it is, it all comes back to the same premise: a promise is made, and if it is kept, the power that is released helps build your business or organization exponentially. If the promise is not kept, that same power will become a destructive force. This is not some philosophical discussion. Where this will ultimately land is your bottom line. Businesses rise and fall according to the answer of this simple question: did my experience as a customer match the promise of the brand? Yes or no?

It doesn't matter if you were first to market, or if you're the largest. It doesn't matter if you think you're the only game in town. You're probably not. In almost every case, there's an alternative for the customer. Even if that alternative means going without the product or service.

Over the past decade, my need to fly for work has taken me from zero status on up the Delta Airlines ladder: Silver, Gold, Platinum, and Diamond Medallion with the added bonus of Million Miler. I spend a fair share of my time in the air.

As with anything, the more time you spend doing something, the more attuned you become to details and to routine. As I was enjoying more and more perks with each level, the baseline continued to rise. What was once extraordinary is now expected. The old ceiling became the new floor.

Packing and going to the airport was not something I dreaded because I knew that my worst-case scenario was priority boarding with a window or aisle seat in premium economy. More often than not, it was in first class, as a free upgrade.

I began to feel like part of the family. I praised Delta every chance I got. I collected fantastic experiences to share with others because my experience matched the promise of being a Diamond Medallion. A dedicated customer service line, first to be upgraded, bonus miles, upgrade certificates, and Sky Club access was the norm.

When Delta changed how one accrues miles for redemption, it had a negative impact on the number of bonus miles I racked up each year. I wrote customer service. I called the Diamond Desk. Everyone was understanding and professional, but it was a business decision and it had been made. It was like that moment when you realize that your parents aren't perfect, or your significant other has a flaw. The honeymoon was decidedly over.

I toyed with the idea of moving to another airline, but the risk felt too great. Since 2001, Delta had been my airline of choice. I had gotten to know them in a very personal way, and I knew the ins and outs that one only discovers after many years. The analogy to a significant other can't be stressed enough here. The relationship was no longer perfect, but on balance, it was still really solid. I decided to stay and am glad I did.

To their credit, Delta actively sought the input of frequent flyers like me for ways they could improve the customer experience, and they followed through. I have new stories of how well I'm treated, and I continue to remain loyal to them, but I'll never have the feeling that I once had. Brand is emotional.

It's also worth noting that though you may be the owner of your brand, once you release it into the wild, your brand lives in the hearts and minds of your customers. That's why what matters most is how your brand lands with your customers, and why you need to be continually seeking consumer input.

WE ARE COLLECTORS
OF EXPERIENCES

We are collectors of experiences. The power of our minds to recall the past in the most vivid details and to envision a future event before it happens is what helps distinguish us as humans. *"Remember when…"* and the floodgates open. Over time, a database of experiences is created that we can access and sort through at a moment's notice. We do it at will when reminiscing. We do it involuntarily, when a word, a smell, a sight, or a shared glance triggers a cascade of feelings. Take a moment now to recall an experience from your past. Fill in all of the details. Allow your senses to make the moment current again. Present time fades away, and the previous experience reoccurs as if it is happening now.

Imagine if a brand is attached to this memory or expectation. Imagine that your most romantic moment in memory occurred at a particular restaurant. Everything seemed to come together that evening in perfect harmony: the ambience, the other diners, the wait staff, the food and beverage, the lighting. From that moment forward, every time you return to that restaurant, that wonderful memory will be evoked, and in some way it will have to live up to that first magical memory.

Conversely, imagine an upsetting recollection, the conjuring of which makes your skin crawl. A client shared an experience of dealing with her auto insurance over a claim for an accident for which she was not at fault. Instead of being assigned someone to manage her case, every time she called back, she was given whoever was available, which meant she had to explain and relive the details of the accident over and over. Once the case settled, she moved to a different insurer.

Then there are experiences that land somewhere between the two extremes. So we not only collect experiences, we curate them.

WE ARE CURATORS OF EXPERIENCES

Like a collection of wine, or art, or stamps, we examine our collections, and select, organize, and care for the items contained within the collection. The best experiences serve multiple purposes. They remind us of how well we've lived, which doesn't necessarily equate to how luxuriously we've lived.

Sure, it could be the five-star restaurant in Paris or the first drive in that Porsche, but more often than not, it's the simple things that evoke the greatest feelings of pleasure. These memories enliven us, particularly when we're feeling down. They give us hope that we'll be able to experience something as good or better in the future.

A friend still talks about the best fish taco he's ever had—twenty years after having eaten it! With the most exquisite detail, he describes how beautiful the day was in Baja California, romanticizing the sight of the surf, the sound of the seagulls, the smell of the salt air. He can still hear the sizzle as the fish hit the grill in the makeshift taco stand, and he rhapsodizes poetically about that first bite. What do we take away from this? Most importantly, the *feeling* the experience left him with.

Another friend recounts how he walked into the hardware store the day after his mom died to get some painting supplies to ready the property for sale. *"The guy behind the counter, whom I hadn't paid much attention to on previous trips, asked if I was OK. He told me that I was always happy when I came in and said I looked a bit down. I lost it, right in the middle of the store. He took me aside, brought me a cup of coffee, and we talked for about ten minutes. I was just buying a can of paint, but I'll always remember both that store and that employee for their compassion, kindness, and caring. And I tell this story every time I can."* Again, the most important takeaway here was the *feeling*.

The best experiences are the ones that we enjoy recounting for friends and recall when we need a lift. They have the power to transport us, effortlessly, and with zero expense. These are the experiences in life that we want to have many more of!

The worst ones serve as a powerful reminder of *"never again."* And when they're associated with a brand, because of the emotional impact that they have, we'll do whatever we can to avoid them, and in so doing, avoid the brand associated with them.

In both cases, because we'll share our experiences with others, brands would do well to give their customers a great story to tell. Not many businesses think in these terms. When someone calls customer support, or goes online to make a purchase, or walks into a store, how many employees are trained to be able to create a positive and memorable story based on the company's promise and the fact that they delivered on it? How often does your team look for places to *"wow"* your customers?

For the sake of argument, let's take the great and the ugly out of the conversation for now. Most people are trained to do the basics: a polite hello, an inquiry about the problem, an earnest attempt to find a solution, an offer to help with the ubiquitous *"anything else,"* and a pleasant thank you and goodbye.

There's not much of a story there. But on those occasions when you connect with someone who has been trained not only to execute the checklist, but also to create a memorable experience, it's magic.

I called my mobile provider to purchase an international pack of data for an upcoming trip to Europe, and during the call she told me that she had done a quick evaluation of my account and could save me about $120 a year by switching to another plan without any penalty. That gave me a great story to tell. And every time my monthly bill arrives (about ten bucks lower than it used to be), I think of her. I also automatically discard all invitations to switch to other providers because of the experience I had and how it made me feel.

So, we remain loyal to the brands that produce the best experiences for us. We stop doing business with brands with whom we have bad experiences. All of this comes back to making a promise and keeping it. It comes back to having integrity.

As we step into the next chapter, it's essential to keep in mind that we cannot change how we are coded, but we can be aware of it. We have survival inscribed in our DNA, and it's because of this that we're here today. As mentioned before, could you imagine if instead of valuing strength, intelligence, and sex appeal, our ancestors had valued cuddling, a good sense of humor, and the ability to dance? We would have lasted one generation at best. So embrace your DNA. Understand that the reflexive responses to the situations we feel threaten us are exactly what allowed us to survive a very harsh world 30,000 years ago. Remember that we crave acceptance because it represents life, and that we hate rejection because it represents death, even to this day.

KEY TAKEAWAYS

- Human beings fear rejection and crave acceptance to the point that rejection equates to death and acceptance equates to life.

- Consequently, we're most easily persuaded by fear because of our survival instinct. An awareness of this gives us access to power.

- Your brand is your promise to your customers.

- Your customer's experience with your brand is their test of whether or not you're telling the truth or lying about your product or service.

- Brand is emotional and experiential.

- We are collectors and curators of experiences, so providing your customers extraordinary experiences gives them things they'll want to repeat and share.

- Conversely, if something in your customer's experience with your brand triggers fear, you are at risk of losing them and having them tell others to avoid you as well.

PUT IT INTO PRACTICE

- Take some time in quiet with pen and paper (yes, pen and paper) and think about experiences you have had with brands, both good and bad.

- Write out the details about one great experience and one bad experience.

- What emotions did they elicit in you?

- How did you feel about the brand after the experience?

- Did you share the experience with others? How, e.g. on social media, in conversation, etc...?

- Did you compliment or complain to the person or company directly? Why or why not?

It's rather amazing that 30,000 years of tribal experience encoded in our DNA is still having an impact on us today. We took a look at why we are the way we are—the biology of being human—and we defined the key topics that we'll be working with throughout the book. You should clearly understand brand promise and customer experience and why we as humans are collectors and curators of experiences.

In the next chapter, we will dive into your brand. Have you defined it? Really? Does your team know what it is? We'll provide plenty of examples and practical exercises you can do to clarify your brand. We'll define key terms like mission, values, and culture. We'll also help you get clear on the importance of a strategic plan—the foundation from which you'll launch your brand.

CHAPTER TWO
DECLARE

You don't have to be a huge company with a massive brand strategy department to determine and declare your brand promise. Anyone can figure it out. After defining your brand promise, it's only a matter of training your team and delivering it to the world. Do this and you'll transform lives.

In 2003, my spouse and I celebrated a Blessing of a Covenant Relationship, a.k.a. a wedding, at St. Thomas the Apostle Church in Hollywood. Marriage equality was ten years away, but we wanted to publicly declare our love for each other and have our priest pronounce God's blessing on our relationship. St. Thomas is an Episcopal Church in the Anglo-Catholic tradition, emphasizing the sacraments and the beauty of worship as well as social justice and inclusion.

Brass, timpani, pipe organ, and a full choir accompanied an hour and a half Solemn High Mass. There was so much incense that the photographer wasn't sure she was going to be able to deliver any clear photos.

One of our guests, a Roman Catholic who hadn't attended Mass in twenty years, felt compelled to receive Holy Communion. In an emotional conversation at the reception, he told me that this was the first time he had felt truly welcomed in church.

St. Thomas understands its brand. It is a place of inclusion where all are invited to take part in the feast. My friend didn't read their website or know anything about the parish before attending. It was simply clear to him that all, truly, are welcome. Because St. Thomas had done the work to understand, declare, map, and train, when it came time to deliver, everything flowed easily and naturally. They didn't have to be something they were not because they were already used to being their brand.

At the reception in the Hancock Park neighborhood of Los Angeles, we thanked our friend, Michael, for allowing us to use his gorgeous home, as well as thanking our friends who had volunteered to help with the ceremony and reception in so many ways.

They all said the same thing: they wanted to do their part to make our wedding a beautiful and unforgettable event. Said differently, they all wanted to make sure we had an experience worth collecting.

***

You can't declare who you are as a brand and know what you're promising your customers unless you define it. In this chapter, we'll do just that: define your brand. I will provide key definitions so we're all singing from the same page, and I will also help you understand why having a strategy matters.

Spoiler alert: companies who plan are more successful than companies who don't.

Here are a few key definitions, as I define them, to open this chapter. Please note that in the world of branding and marketing there are nearly as many definitions as there are consultants, and that's fine. What matters is that however you choose to define these terms, you use them consistently.

- Brand – your promise to your customer
- Culture – how you interact and communicate, internally and externally, based on your values
- Customer Experience – the test of your brand promise
- Mission – what you do, best expressed in a single sentence
- Value – the core of what you stand for, absolute and irreducible

Brand is emotional. Marketing guru Seth Godin defines brand as: *"...the set of expectations, memories, stories and relationships that, taken together, account for a consumer's decision to choose one product or service over another (Godin, 2009)."* As stated in Chapter One, everyone in your company owns your brand, but your brand lives in the experience of your customers.

All of the words used: expectations, memories, stories, and relationships conjure emotions. The words may be based on past experiences, future anticipations, or some combination of the two.

Stop right now. What is your brand? Give it a shot. Define it. What is your promise to your customer? What emotions do you want to evoke in them?

If you know these answers, ask yourself how you're declaring your brand promise to the world? How are you proclaiming who you are? If you don't know, don't worry. There's an exercise coming up in the next few pages that will walk you through the process.

Before we do that, let's return to the topic of emotions. We are feeling beings. We think, most certainly, but we are first and foremost feeling beings that rationalize our choices after they've been made.

A classic example is walking through a big city at night. Imagine that you're strolling down a major thoroughfare. The sights and sounds of the city are everywhere. People surround you, and you feel safe. If something were to go awry, help would be standing by. Police officers are among those in the crowd, adding to a sense of well-being.

You decide to take a shortcut to your hotel, knowing the general direction to follow. In a matter of seconds, the noise and lights fade, and the side street you chose to follow is deserted. In many ways, what you're experiencing reminds you of the opening of far too many horror films. The *"inciting incident"* is only a few pages away!

In the distance, you see another major street. Do you keep going, or do you turn back? You hear something behind you, and without thinking, your pace quickens as you focus on the safety zone ahead.

The once-distant noises become more intense, and you can now hear the sounds of horns honking and the din of people talking. You feel yourself relax as your pace slows, and you finally merge back into the sea of humanity.

As you reflect on what just happened, you congratulate yourself for *"thinking"* things through so clearly. You're impressed with the *"decisions"* you made to keep moving instead of turning back and to walk at a fast (but not too fast) pace, demonstrating your ability to keep calm under pressure.

But the fact is, those decisions were made automatically based on our DNA and survival instincts dating back 30,000 years. This is what your brand is contending with: instant, reflexive responses to stimuli. Hearing a voice when you call customer service that is genuine and caring from the start, being made to feel like you're family when walking into a restaurant, having a digital experience that is so intuitive it seems as though you're gliding without thought toward your purchase, all of these are examples of how to trigger the most desired responses in your prospects and customers.

Most importantly, none of them can be faked. Our instincts are too sophisticated to fall for an act. You know it, intuitively, when it happens. It feels off. It might still be pleasant, but it's not real. It's a performance.

This is most pronounced when calling *"customer care."* If the company representative realizes that every call represents an extraordinary opportunity for their company to learn, course correct, grow through feedback from customers, and responds to your call with appreciation, it's a far different experience than if you feel like you are to blame for having made the call, even if the agent is being polite.

From the perspective of a business owner or employee, complaints should be received as gold. If a customer is willing to take the time to tell you about their bad experience instead of just dropping you, they're indicating a willingness to continue using your brand's services or products. Thank them. Engage them. Own the problem. Apologize for it. Make it right.

Think of the brands you most admire, and why you like them. The product you ordered online arrives on time and in perfect condition. A bartender you met once remembers your drink order when you return one week later. The promised craftsmanship of a handmade item exceeds your expectations. A company simply makes things easy for you.

Whether implied or explicitly stated, the promise of your brand lies at the heart of all these experiences. Only if your promise is delivered in full, every time, at every touchpoint is the promise fulfilled. Remember that whenever a prospect or customer touches your brand—seeing an ad, speaking with a staff member, trying your service or product, visiting your store online or in person, or any number of other examples—they are consciously or subconsciously testing the promise. Your brand, based on how you are, or are not, keeping your promise, will either be enhanced or degraded. There is no neutral. You're telling the truth or you're lying.

Over time, those great or slight enhancements or degradations will either accrue to your benefit or detriment. And there will come a tipping point for either success or failure.

How do you go about defining your brand? What is the promise that you are making to the world? The world may not be your target market, but thinking globally will open you to far bigger possibilities than you've previously imagined.

At the heart of what you're embarking on is a quest to understand not only your product or service in the most complete way you can, but also to understand the potential impact that it can have on society. If you can get to that point, then you can better craft your brand promise and make that the touchstone of your work.

It's easy to understand how a heart monitor or an anti-cancer medication could be considered impactful or life-changing. But the stakes needn't be as high as the possibility of curing cancer. Most of our experiences are far gentler, even mundane. So what about a cheese grater or a water bottle?

Ridiculous examples? Not at all. We welcome simple things that make our daily lives easier. We love stuff that solves a problem, works well, and makes us feel good. As you identify the promise and consider the positive impact that your product or service can have on people's lives, you'll also want to get customer feedback about how your brand is playing out in practice.

Why do people feel the way they do about interacting with your brand? You certainly want to know the answers, whether they are positive or negative. It's only input, so don't put a value judgment on the information that you're receiving. Welcome it all.

You want to know why people are feeling good about your brand so you can replicate those experiences and you most definitely want to know where you're missing the mark so you can correct course. Once you can accurately communicate your brand promise and deliver it consistently via a superior customer experience, you'll be building the most valuable commodity of all: Trust.

Trust works something like your GPA: so difficult for it to increase, yet so easy for it to crumble.

For business women and men who travel, think of some of the different components that make up your day. The airlines—you're literally trusting a couple of people in the cockpit with your life and the lives of hundreds of other people. Hotels—you're trusting people to give you a safe, clean, and comfortable place to lay your head. Restaurants—you're trusting someone to nourish you with good food that is sanitary.

Living in the desert Southwest, most people dress pretty casually. *"Dressed up"* for me implies a button-down shirt. During the hot months of summer, one of the great debates I had with myself in the mirror every morning was whether or not to tuck my shirt in. Did I look too casual with the shirt untucked or not? No matter what choice I initially made, an hour or two into the day, I would inevitably wish I'd made a different decision. If the shirt was already tucked in, I couldn't very well untuck it—people would see the wrinkles. If the shirt was left out and then tucked in later, it seemed as though I was absent-minded, forgetting to tuck in my shirt at the beginning of the day.

While in New York City for business a couple of years ago, I was wandering the streets in lower Manhattan and came across a storefront called *"Untuckit"* and went inside. It was as though a chorus of angels had begun to sing. The store had rack after rack of shirts that were designed to be worn untucked. They were tailored to the appropriate length, and looked as though they were meant to be worn without being tucked in. Just like the brand said.

Was it a new cancer fighting medication? No. But I walked out of the store feeling better about how I looked than I had in a couple of years. I found myself standing taller, feeling less self-conscious, and being more present to what was happening in the moment, including being able to easily give my undivided attention to the people I was talking to without wondering about the *"to tuck or not to tuck"* decision I had made that day.

In talking with one of the sales reps, I recognized his passion for what they had created, and it resonated with me. He knew that he was providing men with more than a shirt. He was providing them with self-confidence.

Whatever your product, whatever your service, you owe it to yourself to take seriously what you're offering the public.

A friend of mine sells very inexpensive giveaway items, things like magnets and pens that you commonly find as *"bait"* at trade shows. They are of no great value in and of themselves. But what they do provide is attraction. The items bring prospects to his customers' booths. My friend showed me the statistics of booth inquiries and sales at trade shows with and without offering *"swag,"* as they call it in the business.

The results are stunning. Some pens, a bowl full of stress balls, or glow in the dark stickers for business men and women to take home to their kids is all it really takes. Regardless of the exact nature of the giveaway, the result is that my friend is able to provide an inexpensive, reliable way to attract more booth traffic and ultimately more leads and sales compared to booths with no giveaways.

He doesn't consider himself a *"swag"* salesman. He thinks of himself as the precursor that helps draw prospects to the booths of his clients. As he told me, *"When I have a medical device company as a client, I see myself as an extension of the sales team for whatever they're selling, like a heart monitor. My products are the invitations that give people permission to approach the booth. They don't know the role I play, but that doesn't matter. It gives me a lot of pride knowing that I can be part of something bigger."*

DETERMINING YOUR BRAND PROMISE

Though brand is emotional and also determined by how you want people to feel when they interact with it, consider the following key factors to help you know your brand:

1. Why does your company do what it does? Simon Sinek has one of the best videos that I've seen on this topic. Most often, we begin with what, then move to how, and finally, if we even know it, to why. His premise, start with *"why"* is profound (Sinek, 2009).

2. What are the core values that your company has which are absolute and irreducible? How are those values translated into your brand?

3. What is the benefit to your customers if they choose you?

4. How is your company distinguished from the competition? In other words, why you?

5. How does your company contribute to others?

LET'S TAKE A DEEPER LOOK AT EACH OF THESE ITEMS:

What's Your Why?

This is the most overlooked step in the process of determining brand. Sometimes it's useful to begin with the *"lower order"* features and benefits. Here's an example.

Let's say you're manufacturing an anti-HIV medication that previously required three doses a day, but you've been able to reformulate it to be just as effective with a single dose a day. That's the objective, verifiable feature of your product.

The functional benefit is convenience. If someone who had to stop three times a day to think about taking a pill, and, more importantly, to be reminded that they're living with HIV, could reduce that experience by 66%, that's an extraordinary benefit. The highest order benefit, as you might have suspected, is a feeling. The patient feels in control. She feels like the burden of dealing with this disease is reduced because it's a single daily occurrence. It's now manageable.

Your *"why"* and the customer's highest experience are matched. Why did you manufacture this single-dose medication? To give your patients the feeling of being in control. Why do your patients buy your medication? Because they want to feel in control. Your brand promise to your customers is to put them in control. To give them power. To make them the boss. Notice that the brand promise doesn't mention anything about fighting HIV or even that this is a medication. It's all about restoring control. A reminder that brand, at its core, is emotional and experiential.

The challenge in considering these deepest-level questions is to avoid the temptation to create a laundry list of what you do, or even how you do it. You'll need to consider those, without a doubt, but not as the first step.

Core Values

Your company will change and transform over time, but your values should remain constant, absolute, and irreducible. Your core values speak to the character of your brand. The foundation, the touchstone, the North Star—whatever metaphor you wish to use—is what anchors your company, particularly during tough times.

When your company grows from just a few people whom you have lunch with every day to a company so large that you occupy an entire floor in a skyscraper, going days without seeing your colleagues in person, your core values will hold you together. The same holds true for virtual offices. Core values unite people without the need for them to be in the same space.

Your values will shape your culture, they will guide your hiring, and they will help you determine the kinds of clients that you want to do business with. So, ask yourself: what are the values that you want associated with your brand?

A word of caution: please don't view this as a *"throwaway"* exercise. You need to know your values, and I recommend posting them on your website. After my homepage and my blog, my *"About"* page, which contains my core values, is the most visited page on my site. It really does matter.

Customer Benefit

This is a broad look at your product or service through the lens of a customer or prospect. What's in it for them? What's the benefit that they're going to derive by purchasing what you're selling?

I use a whiteboard or big sticky notes for this process by writing every top-level benefit I can think of, and then in cascade fashion, every second-level and third-level benefit that flows from the primary one.

By way of example, airports are starting to use automated boarding gates, meaning the passenger scans her own ticket, the gate opens, and she boards. Let's make the assumption that you're the CEO of a company manufacturing these automated gates.

If you think about how boarding usually works at US airports, there are one or two gate agents who are responsible for all the activity from the arrival of the inbound flight to the departure of the outbound flight: making announcements on the public-address system, dealing with special needs such as unaccompanied minors and wheelchair requests, fielding questions from passengers, checking excess baggage, delivering it to the ramp agents, answering the phone and intercom, and scanning tickets.

Automated boarding gates free up the gate agents from the single most monotonous and time-consuming task: scanning tickets. The agents are now free to focus on the needs of passengers at the gate. According to the PwC survey mentioned in an earlier chapter, 82 percent of US customers want more human interaction as technology evolves. What's the top-level benefit? The freedom that automated gates give customer service agents to focus on passenger needs.

What's a second-level benefit that flows from increased attention to passenger needs? Passengers have a more personalized and thoughtful experience with the gate agent because the agent is not trying to multitask.

Continuing the cascade of benefits, a passenger who feels cared for, particularly during the stressful boarding experience, will feel more relaxed. They now board the aircraft in a better mood, which contributes a sense of calm to the cabin.

Do this as many times as you can, until you have an exhaustive list. Don't get overly concerned about ranking. Just think in terms of flow, and what benefit logically follows another.

Why You?

Think of this as your value proposition, or your value add. You know what the benefits are to your customers. But it's entirely possible that your competitors have virtually the same list. So narrow it down.

What distinguishes you from the competition? Are you doing something that others aren't by filling a need that no one else is addressing? Perhaps you're doing the same thing that others are, but you're doing it differently. Maybe you're doing it better, or offering something of higher quality, or at a lower price? Are you giving a guarantee where others are not? Maybe you have a superior level of customer support such as offering an online chat solution in addition to email.

What ultimately matters is that you're able to frame your company in a way that separates it from your competitors and elevates it above them. But the focus needs to be the *"above and beyond"* that you provide. Not what your competition lacks.

Being a contribution

This takes some thought. How is your company contributing to making life on the planet better? It could be the product or service you offer. It could be the community service work that your team engages in. Maybe one of your core values is kindness, and your goal is to make someone smile each day. Maybe you have a commitment to being a green company or having a LEED Certified building.

It may be some combination of these items and it may be something that I haven't listed. Take the time to inquire. It will be worth the effort.

***

Once you know why you do what you do, the core values that are sacrosanct, and how you differentiate yourself from the competition, you're ready to discuss your brand promise.

Here are a few examples of famous brand promises. Some of them mention the product or service that they provide. Others do not. For some, their brand promise is also their tag line. Keep in mind that brand is generally customer facing, and that mission is generally company facing.

- Geico: *"15 minutes or less can save you 15% or more on car insurance."*
- Coors Light: *"The World's Most Refreshing Beer."*
- Coca-Cola: *"To inspire moments of optimism and uplift."*
- BMW: *"The Ultimate Driving Machine."*
- Nike: *"To bring inspiration and innovation to every athlete in the world."*
- Harley Davidson: *"We are Harley Davidson."*
- The NFL: *"To be the premier sports and entertainment brand that brings people together, connecting them socially and emotionally like no other."*
- Apple: *"Think different."*
- Starbucks: *"To inspire and nurture the human spirit – one person, one cup and one neighborhood at a time."*
- Marriott: *"Quiet luxury. Crafted experiences. Intuitive service."*
- Walmart: *"Save money. Live better."*

Whether the promise mentions the product or service or not, it is reflective of something much bigger, something which evokes a feeling, a deep emotion. *"Evoke"* is a term that you should dwell on in this process. You're literally working on crafting something that calls forth a feeling that provokes, excites, comforts, enlivens, or calms, to name but a few. That's how big this is.

Here are some suggestions about getting to the heart of the promise of your brand. There's no magic here. *"After enlightenment comes the dishes."* You understand—it's work.

Note that this process is not specific to creating your brand promise. It provides a frame that you can use for virtually any kind of collaboration you can think of.

Here are the main components:

- Gather key members of your team
- Collect information
- Crunch the data
- Make a decision

First, if you have an existing company, gather a few staff members to form a task force. A task force is different than a committee because the task force comes together for a specific time and a specific purpose, and then disbands. Too many companies have too many *"committees"* that exist without a defined purpose or a defined period. This work needs to be done with care, but it also needs to be done with speed.

If you have a substantial-sized staff, bring in a mix of people from administration to C-Suite level. If you don't, improvise. If you're a one-person shop, reach out to trusted and respected colleagues who you know will tell you the truth and ask them to serve on the task force. Five is an ideal number. If you're the owner of a company, and your presence might prevent others from speaking freely, you may want to consider being somewhat removed from the process initially, so that others don't feel intimidated. It's also a challenge to be objective about your own business or a business or organization that you're leading, so use your best judgment now that you're aware of the challenges.

Second, be upfront in letting people know the commitment by defining the specific work of the task force and the period of time it will take to complete its work. Here is a process I've used and recommend:

1. Create a list of people to interview
2. Create a list of questions appropriate for the interviewees
3. Conduct the interviews
4. Synthesize the information
5. Report back with your insights

Who should you interview? You want to interview both those inside and outside of the company, including:

1. employees
2. prospective employees
3. current customers
4. former customers
5. shareholders or board members, if you have them

If you're just getting started, interview prospective customers.

Picture a funnel when creating the questionnaire. A question as broad as, *"What does Acme Co. do?"* or *"What kind of business is Acme Co.?"* can yield truly insightful results because seemingly obvious questions give us a glimpse into how our organization is perceived by both those within it and those in the outside world.

Work your way down from there, thinking of each of the demographic groups you're going to interview.

Examples include asking customers why they walked in the door or visited your site online to begin with. If they're repeat customers, ask why they've stayed with you. Perhaps your prices are higher than the competitors, so why aren't they going somewhere else? Was it the customer service? The extraordinary user experience online? The quality of the product you're producing?

If you have access to former clients and customers, why did they leave you? This information can be equally, if not more, useful and can yield surprising results. A client for whom we did this work reported that one of their ongoing customers left because as the company grew, the personalized emails stopped. She loved that connection more than she loved the product, and once the connection—the relationship—was gone, then where she purchased the product became superfluous.

If you're in the initial stages of launching a business, ask about current pain points for prospective customers. What relief are they looking for? What do they want in the particular product or service that you're going to be offering that they cannot find elsewhere? What do they want in their shopping and buying experience? What would make them switch from where they're currently buying to your brand?

It's important that these interviews be done on the phone or in person. A seemingly simple *"why is that?"* can yield far more results than you could ever hope to get from a written questionnaire. When you hear a person's voice, you can hear silences, nuanced speech, hesitations, a deep breath, etc....

All of these vocal cues, if you're paying attention, provide an opening to go deeper. An effective strategy is to state what you heard, for example, *"You've been answering all the questions so easily, but this one seemed to cause you to pause. Can you tell me what this brings up for you?"*

Most people want to be asked their opinion. They want to feel like their voice matters and that perhaps, if taken seriously, it could produce change. If someone doesn't want to answer, they'll tell you. When I worked in various positions as a development director, my mentor told me that no one would ever give away their last dime to charity, so ask. The same applies here. Ask. If they don't want to tell you, they won't.

If you have a board of directors or advisers, what inspires them to give of their time? And if you're a non-profit, what inspires them to give of their money? Why would they want to identify with your brand?

Ask employees why they've come to work for you when they could have gone elsewhere. If you have resumes or applications on hand for future employment, ask why someone would want to work for you. And if someone quit for employment elsewhere, and you're able to reach them, what led to their departure?

There is rich insight to be found in all of these answers. And in each of them, how the client, or employee, or shareholder feels, is of paramount importance.

At the conclusion of the interviews, the task force should meet up and discuss the answers. Though I usually think that distributing information in advance is useful, in this case, there's something powerful about experiencing the reactions of your colleagues for the first time and using your now finely-honed interview skills on each other. I'm a huge proponent of using a whiteboard or multiple giant, sticky flip charts to begin teasing out common findings, and interesting disparate ones as well.

There are plenty of famous examples of brand promises out there. What I urge you to do is trust your feelings. The task force should craft three to five possible brand promise statements and test them with the people whom you've interviewed and with everyone in the company. If you've done your interviews well, and thoughtfully considered your options, the only thing that should remain is fine-tuning.

Remember, the brand does NOT have to specifically mention the product or service that you offer. It only needs to evoke the emotion that you want from prospects and customers, and the genuine promise that you and your company will be absolutely focused on delivering.

Ultimately, your focus is not to create a brand promise that is intellectually understood, but rather one that is viscerally felt.

The goal, after declaring your brand, is to see and hear comments like *"it felt GREAT to be in their store,"* or *"I felt as though someone was guiding me through the simplest order process online"* or *"I felt safe when I clicked the 'purchase' button,"* or *"I don't know the person who helped me at the reception desk, but I've never felt so welcomed!"* It goes without saying, but I'll say it anyway: no promise will be worth anything if your product or service itself isn't great.

Implicit in all of this is that customers, whether interacting with you online, on the phone, or in person, will simply *"get"* your promise. They will see your values in action. They'll know who you are, and just as importantly who you are NOT. They will feel the *"why"* of what you do.

A STRATEGIC PLAN

"When you fail to plan, you plan to fail," as Benjamin Franklin is reported to have said. It seems reasonable since he was obsessed with time management. As important as a plan is, the primary benefit of strategic planning isn't just the plan itself. It's the result of what happens when stakeholders come together, often for the first time, to work as a team.

Strategic planning also serves another purpose: that of building a solid foundation from which to tell your brand story.

When I'm leading strategic planning engagements with organizations, we explore in-depth the reasons why your company exists, and we take stock of your strengths and weaknesses, recording where your team is aligned and where they're not. This intense engagement provides every participant with the experience of contributing to the creation of a shared vision of the future, and then uniting to accomplish it.

One of my clients famously likened strategic planning to something that Stalin would enjoy, which helped me to realize that this business procedure is not universally loved. My process consists of five phases, and you can take this on as a company, with or without an outside consultant.

What's the advantage of hiring a consultant to guide you? You can stay focused on the work, and not worry about the process.

To help you with this, check out my free training video at: Mosesian.com/promise

HERE'S AN OVERVIEW

Phase One: Initiation and Discovery

In working with clients, I have them create a strategy task force (STF) to lead the process. It's called a task force and not a committee for a reason. A task force comes together, for a limited time, to perform a specific task, and then disbands. It's important, particularly when asking people to take on additional work, that they know this is not an assignment that will last into perpetuity. Depending on the size and the willingness of the company, we'll tap key people from diverse departments to bring as many perspectives to the table as is practical.

From there, it's on to reviewing performance data from the past three to five years, creating an interview schedule with current and past clients, current and past employees, board members (if applicable), and other key stakeholders. A timeline and deliverables map for the planning process is produced. That means creating specific measurable results, to be accomplished by specific dates, with one person responsible for each main result.

I've found it useful to channel most all communication through the STF. It gives the members a sense of ownership, they bond quickly as a team, and all involved seem to treat peer-to-peer requests with respect and to follow through with completing them. This is the Honeymoon Phase. People are excited, change is in the air, and it feels like all things are possible. It won't last, and that's actually a good thing.

Phase Two: Baseline Assessment

From the perspective of pure pleasure, a term that most people have never associated with strategic planning, this phase is my favorite. And why is that? A very good question! Because in Phase Two, there is invariably low-hanging fruit to be harvested.

And it comes from the interviews with key stakeholders.

In a perfect world, this group of stakeholders includes current and past employees, current and past customers, board members (if you have them) and anyone else with a stake in the success of the company. As constructive as all of the interviews are, it's the ones with current and past customers that I find the most enlightening, usually because of their simplicity:

- *"They finished the project, and then never contacted me again. I had two additional projects, but their lack of interest turned me off."*
- *"They never told me that they had expanded their product offering. I would have purchased from them, but I didn't know that they now carried what I needed."*
- *"I get that we're all busy, but take me out for a cup of coffee a couple of times a year for no other reason than to connect with me."*
- *"All they have to do is call. I have work waiting."*

Inevitably, this allows me to recommend how we can quickly harvest said low-hanging fruit. Not only is this appreciated by the client, but it demonstrates to stakeholders that your company listens and responds. This is also a time to analyze and report trends, and we integrate past performance data into the assessment along with the interview results to provide the most accurate picture of what's so at this moment in time.

Phase Three: Vision and Strategic Goals

The honeymoon is over. Which is not a bad thing. Solid relationships founded on trust and mutual respect grow, deepen, and strengthen when you realize that your husband, wife, partner, parent, clergy person—you get the idea—is not perfect and that you have legitimate differences of opinion.

It's the same with organizations. Strategic planning, done well, is meant to honestly assess not only your company's strengths and weaknesses, but also how closely your team is aligned in terms of their shared vision for the future. It calls for deep thinking, for a willingness to be moved from individual positions, and for compromise.

Note that I said *"solid relationships founded on trust and mutual respect."* Strategic planning can act like a stress test for a company, and without a solid foundation, there is nothing on which to build.

> **As stated above, the primary benefit of strategic planning isn't just the plan itself. It's the result of what happens when stakeholders come together, often for the first time, to work as a team.**

During this phase, led by the Strategy Task Force, we'll review—or create—the vision, mission, and values of the company, discuss how to make them come alive in the day-to-day work of the organization, and generate no more than five strategic goals designed to advance the mission.

All of this is summarized in a document that defines the future of the company, and that document will serve as a roadmap for our next phase where we'll create and implement the plan.

Phase Four: Create and Implement Plans and Launch

Almost there! This phase begins with a review of each of the four to five strategic goals that were created. A task force will be named for each goal, and a team lead appointed. We'll determine the desired end result—what constitutes success—for each one. Then we'll work backwards, developing the actions necessary to arrive at those results.

Remember that we defined a task force as a group that comes together to accomplish a specific task in a specific period of time, and then disbands. This is a critically important point to make when assembling your teams. People can enjoy their work together to a far greater degree when they know that they signed up for a limited-time engagement.

A timeline with deliverables will be established, so that we have a defined path to follow and so we will know, at any given point, if we're on time and on task or if we need to make a course correction.

I'm a big believer in the power of ceremonial actions to memorialize important occasions, so I ask every team member to sign off on the plan. It cements in people's minds that they're in this together, that everyone has some part to play in its success, and that they're agreeing to the direction of the company.

Phase Five: Evaluation and Course Correction

"After enlightenment comes the dishes"—or so the saying goes. For many companies, the strategic planning process is something that produces insights that otherwise would have gone unnoticed. While these peak experiences feel great, it's time to come down from the mountain and do the dishes, or chop the wood, or any number of other expressions that simply mean it is time to go to work.

It's essential, particularly during the first ninety days, to check in regularly and frequently. I recommend 30-day intervals so you're never too far away from a course correction if you need to make one. Why should you be making course corrections? Because a strategic plan is not something set in stone. It is meant to be a living, breathing, dynamic document. Ask the most basic questions: Where are you relative to where you should be? Where are you succeeding? Where are you failing? Why?

Two years after I completed a plan with a large national organization, I stopped in to visit the CEO. She had a copy of the plan printed out and sitting on her desk. It was marked up with notes in the margins and had yellow highlights throughout. Pages were dog-eared, and it looked like a well-used book.

They took their plan seriously, and it showed. What was the outcome of their strategic planning process? Why did they bother to do it in the first place?

For her, it gave their organization a point of focus. It gave them attainable goals. It gave them instructions on how to direct their resources. And it taught them how to work together as a team at a far more effective level than before.

Most strategic plans, as outlined above, take a solid three to nine months to complete. Having said that, you can do a quick start variant in a day. It's another service I offer, a Day of Discovery and Action, and it's designed to help you and your team gain insights and produce breakthroughs, no matter the topics.

Whatever route you choose, and whether you have someone assist you or not, invest the time to create a plan. There's just no substitute for it, and you need this foundation from which to launch or relaunch your brand.

✳✳✳

I can think of no better personal example to illustrate a company knowing their brand than the following one. Yes, it's about my first colonoscopy. But I promise, other than the word itself, there is no description of the actual procedure!

A few years back, I had a standoff with my physician. I had never had a colonoscopy, and being the age that I was, particularly with a history of cancer in my family, he told me to get one done before my next physical, as I was long overdue. He gave me a list of preferred providers who all accepted my insurance. He told me the importance of early intervention if something was discovered and how time is never on your side in terms of diagnosing colon cancer. After three years of avoiding this procedure, my doctor also gave me an ultimatum: have the colonoscopy done or find a new primary care physician. I decided to make good on my word and follow through.

What followed was a textbook example of extraordinary customer experiences, which built trust at every turn.

I did some research online, liked the reviews that I read about one particular practice, and then went to their website. It felt friendly and professional. There were photos of the MDs and bios that were meaningful to me as a patient. The site was simple to navigate and intuitive. They outlined what the procedure was all about, and what specifically my experience would be like on the day that I arrived for the colonoscopy.

I called. A person answered the phone. She took all of my information and scheduled the procedure. She asked about my preference for a pharmacy and emailed me instructions to access the patient portal on their site.

She then told me what would happen next. The prep kit would be ordered and sent to the pharmacy. She would track it and call me when it arrived so I could pick it up. She told me she'd also call back the next day to make sure I had retrieved it. A couple of weeks later, one of the nurses would call the day before I was to begin the prep and walk me through the instructions.

Just like she promised, I got a call informing me that the kit was at the pharmacy, and just like she promised, she called me to confirm that I had picked it up. A few weeks later, the day before I was to begin my prep, the nurse called. She walked me through the prep instructions and reviewed the dietary restrictions as well.

On the morning of the procedure, my spouse and I drove to the office. Never having had a colonoscopy before, I brought a box of See's Candy for the staff. It made for a great icebreaker!

The office was located in a corporate park, but one that was landscaped and well-maintained. The office itself was beautiful, and once my ID was checked and paperwork reviewed, the nurse met me and then guided me into one of the exam rooms.

It too was beautiful. Artwork hung on the walls. The floors were gleaming. The furniture was new, the mirrors were clean, and the sink was immaculate.

My nurse explained everything that was going to happen next, which, by the way, matched the story on their website exactly. Literally at every step they were building trust and confidence in their brand because they were keeping their promise with every action.

The doctor came in to meet me, discussed the procedure, and asked if I had any questions. We talked about the big, fat elephant in the room—Cancer—the reason I had avoided the procedure all along, as if not knowing would somehow make cancer go away if it was there. The absurdity of this story is made richer by the fact that I was an EMT in an ER for several years, so this was all familiar territory to me.

The doctor took the time to have an honest, yet reassuring conversation with me, and I actually felt that if the news I got was bad, I could handle it.

After he left, I changed into a gown, and the nurse returned, started my IV, drew my blood, and called for a gurney. I was wheeled into the OR, and the anesthesiologist carefully explained the type of anesthesia that would be used and how quickly I would come up and out of my sleep. They also asked if I wanted my husband in the recovery room when I came to.

Then it was count backwards time, and the next thing I remember was waking up in the recovery area. Bob was at my side, and my nurse had a cranberry juice for me. The doctor came in and said, *"You don't have cancer."*

Besides the extraordinary gratitude that I felt upon hearing those words, I was truly appreciative that he didn't walk me through the entire procedure first, saving the end result for last. This was one of those times that I wanted to flip to the back of the book and read the last page! The next day, I got a call from one of the staff members to see how I was feeling.

The day after that, I got a call from one of the staff members to ask me if there was anything that they could have done to better serve me.

Now, I realize that you most likely didn't pick up this book to read about the author's colonoscopy. But I hope you see the value in relating the story in such detail. This practice understood that most people coming in for this procedure only have one thing, and one thing only, on their minds: they want to know if they have cancer.

Even though colon cancer is highly treatable, it's still cancer. It's a word that strikes fear in the heart of anyone who hears it. So from the beginning they did everything possible to mitigate fear and to inspire trust. How did they do that? By keeping the promises that they made, relentlessly, every time they made one.

Because I believe in the Rule of Three's, a *"promise"* doesn't require you to say *"I promise."* That's what a five-year-old says.

If you say you will do something, you've made a promise.

If you advertise a feature or quality of your product or service, you've made a promise.

If you make a claim, you've made a promise.

You'll either keep your promise, or you won't.

You'll tell the truth, or you'll lie.

It really is that simple.

In my experience, I was not only dealing with my own fear of cancer. My mom died of colon cancer. Both my mother-in-law died of breast cancer and my father-in-law died of colon cancer.

I was walking into that office with the collective experiences that I had in dealing with my family. Yet every time they told me that they would do something, and then did it, my fear ebbed and my trust grew.

They didn't make any far-fetched claims. There was no false hope given. But somehow, just knowing that I was dealing with people of integrity allowed me to breathe. They knew that brand is emotional. They understood that as beings focused on survival, we're constantly surveying the environment, looking for danger. And what they managed to do was remove any signs of risk, allowing me to focus on the great experience that they were creating: the attractiveness of the building inside and out, the kindness of the language that the staff used, the flow that I felt from start to finish.

The icing on the cake, was the follow up call. *"Is there anything that we could have done that would have made your experience better?"*

I have told this story in every retreat I've led. I've told it in coaching sessions. And now I'm sharing it in this book. That is the power of promise.

It may simply be a feeling of comfort or pleasure. It may be as powerful as knowing that regardless of the outcome of a significant medical test, you're in good hands. Brand is emotional and feelings are feedback.

KEY TAKEAWAYS:

- Brand is emotional.

- Know what emotions you want your brand to evoke in your customers—what you want them to feel.

- Trust lies at the heart of every good customer experience.

- If you say something, it constitutes a promise. *"I didn't say 'I promise'"* is the refuge of a five-year-old. You're not a five-year-old. Actually, if you're a five-year-old, please call me immediately. I want to meet you!

- Key questions to ask when formulating your brand:
  - Why do you do what you do?
  - What are your core values?
  - How is your company different from the competition?
  - How does your product or service benefit your customer?
  - What is unique about what you provide?
  - How is your company a contribution to others?

- *"When you fail to plan, you plan to fail,"* as Benjamin Franklin is reported to have said. Companies with a strategic plan do better than those who don't have one.

- After every enlightening retreat, it's time to do the dishes. Or chop the wood. Whatever the expression, it's time to go to work.

PUT IT INTO PRACTICE

Gather your team and walk through the exercise outlined on pages 50-60, *"Determining Your Brand Promise."* Even if you're not at a place to do the entire exercise, at least complete the first section, Key Factors:

- Why do you do what you do?
- What are your core values?
- How is your company different from the competition?
- How does your product or service benefit your customer?
- What is unique about what you provide?
- How is your company a contribution to others?

There you have it. Your brand, defined. And you now understand why having a strategic plan matters, that it takes a few months to create, but that a quick start variant can be done in a day.

You should also be conversant in the language of brand promise, customer experience, mission, values, and culture, and have a good sense of how important touchpoints are for your customers on their way to becoming advocates for your brand. Remember, don't make yourself crazy regarding definitions; just be consistent in how you use each term.

In the next chapter, we'll provide a detailed example of a customer's journey, mapping each and every touchpoint along the way. In so doing, you will gain a place from which to create your own customer experience map because your customer's journey should never be left to chance. The more details you can anticipate, the better an experience you can provide. And you should always be reviewing the map, taking into account customer and staff feedback, and making appropriate adjustments.

CHAPTER THREE
MAP

Every one of your actions affects your brand. The impact can extend beyond the obvious, and have second-level ramifications that are seldom considered. It's a good reminder about reviewing processes and asking what the consequences will be for your customers, both intended and unintended.

***

A friend shared that eighteen months after his dad died, he received a bill from the ambulance company addressed to his father in the amount of $2,500. He was filled with rage, but not primarily at the size of the bill. Instead, he was angry at the fact that after a year and a half of working through his dad's death and making peace with it, this bill resurrected all of the pain and heartache, in the most jarring way.

"I was going through the mail, not really paying much attention, and then—this! I hit the roof. How can anyone do business this way?

It makes no sense financially. And I kept thinking this is the worst customer service I've ever experienced. They have no idea how much this hurt me."

To my friend, it was much more than a bill. It was a reminder of his dad's last ride while he was alive on earth. Had it arrived in the first few months after his dad's death, with the bills from the hospital and the physicians, it would have been received differently.

But it didn't. There was no note attached to the bill, no apology, no attempt to connect on a human level.

The power of promise is about companies understanding that what they do is bigger than their product or service because they are dealing with their fellow human beings. It's also a stark reminder that no matter how good the service may have been along the way, one significant misstep can do equally significant damage to your brand.

***

This chapter is all about you putting yourself in the shoes of your customer. I'll give you a detailed example of what it takes to make the journey BEFORE your customer does so you can anticipate the pitfalls and correct for them. This will also help you look for touchpoints that provide an opportunity to enhance your customer's experience.

Done well, this is the elite realm of customer service. This is about creating raving fans for your brand; they become advocates and ambassadors. At my mom's funeral, the mortuary director told us we had carried out a service with more grace and dignity than she had seen in her entire career. We knew, as odd as it may sound, that we had provided my dad an *"elite"* customer experience in giving my mom a send-off worthy of that compliment.

It's essential that baseline measures be taken, as objectively as possible, to give you a starting point against which to measure progress. If you don't know where you are, you can't chart a course to where you want to be.

For this example, let's make a few assumptions. Let's assume you have a physical store. A café, to be exact. You don't have to own a café for this exercise to be effective. It is simply a frame for you to work with to create your own map. As you read through this, do so from the perspective of your own business, paying particular attention to the levels of detail. For every step your customer takes, there are oftentimes multiple outcomes. Ask *"what if?"* or *"what then?"* at every point as you think this through. Take notes. Use a whiteboard. Do whatever is necessary to memorialize your work. Do it with a few other people as you create your map.

Let's assume that the person who's going to lead us through this exercise is a prospect who has heard of you via an ad, but they've never been to your store. As you'll read in the example, you start at whatever constitutes the beginning for your business. If you operate solely online, you need to start with how someone searches for you, and the user experience they have from the moment your site appears on their device. First impressions matter. Can you capture their attention immediately when there are millions of rabbit holes waiting to be explored? Aw, cute puppy! And they're gone.

If you own a brick and mortar business, everything that a prospect or customer encounters en route to your store will be part of the collective body of evidence that they are stockpiling, which will then be used to judge you and your brand.

That bias is in part a product of how they found you—a drive, a walk, the bus, a bike, or the metro. You may not be able to control these factors, but you can be sensitive to them.

Once they do arrive, what does the storefront look like? Is there a garage or parking lot? Is it nicely paved and well lit? Are the grounds clean, the building painted? What about the signage? Is it clear and inviting?

If you're located in an upscale area of town, people may feel priced out before they enter your establishment if they see high-end cars on the street. If you're located in an *"up and coming"* area of town, they may feel uncomfortable, even unsafe, getting to your store.

What happens when a prospect walks in the door? They are walking in with a judgment of who you are even before the first *"hello."*

So, what's a business owner to do? Plan. Anticipate. Listen. Be present. Every prospect is a potential customer. Every customer is a potential fan, advocate, and ambassador.

Our prospect, Martha, saw an ad that touted the good food at your café. She's working in a new job in a part of town that's close to your business. In looking at the address, Martha realized that it's not a part of town she would feel comfortable in at night, but hey, it's *"up and coming"* and *"trendy"* and *"hip"* and *"what's next,"* so what the heck? Besides, she's going for lunch, so everything should be fine.

Martha likes being on the cutting edge of the food and beverage scene, and it would be great to again discover someplace new to share with her friends. The drive to your café does not inspire confidence, but Martha is willing to look beyond the surroundings in hopes of a great meal for lunch.

When she arrives, she finds herself in a warehouse district. Yes, it's *"up and coming,"* but the newer businesses are few and far between. There are some deserted buildings and others that have almost no activity.

It crosses Martha's mind that maybe she should have driven in the opposite direction and gone to her tried and true lunch spot. As much as she likes discovering what's next, she also loves feeling safe and at home. Even though it's the noon hour, she still has an uncomfortable feeling.

The parking lot is riddled with potholes, and walking from the lot into the café makes Martha feel uneasy. Once inside, Martha discovers only a few patrons. The staff is hustling behind the counter in the back of the café. There's a hostess stand in the front, but it's unclear if she should seat herself or wait, and there's no signage indicating what to do.

Martha decides to have a seat. After a few minutes, someone behind the counter signals for her to come up. She's told that there's no table service at lunch, and she needs to order at the counter.

OK. But there's no menu or menu board to order from. The staff member has disappeared into the kitchen so Martha calls out and someone emerges. *"I need a menu, please."* The staff member grabs a menu and drops it on the counter only to disappear again.

A moment later, another staff person emerges and asks Martha if she's ready yet. Martha wants to ask about the details of one of the sandwiches, but given how the first few minutes have progressed, she just orders and takes a seat.

Looking around, the café looks dilapidated, and not in an ironic way. They've only been at this location for a few weeks so maybe they just didn't have the time or resources yet to make the needed upgrades. But something in Martha's mind wonders about how sanitary the kitchen is given that the table she's sitting at has not been wiped down since the last patron was there. She requests that a server take care of that, which he quickly does.

The room smells like soup, which is good, but also smells kind of musty, which is bad. Martha is put off by a small patch of peeling paint, again thinking about what the food prep area is like. She pulls out her phone hoping for free Wi-Fi, but there's none. She thinks about how nice that would have been.

As an aside, most of us were taught not to be judgmental, but it's impossible. We are, by design, always evaluating everything in our surroundings based on our hardwired desire for survival. We continually ask ourselves on conscious and subconscious levels if something is good for us or bad for us. We judge. It's who we are.

Combine this DNA-based judgment with the evaluative process that we use to determine our feelings about a brand, and there is no escaping the scrutiny that we apply, consciously and subconsciously, to every situation we encounter.

Back at the café, Martha notices that the staff members are talking with each other in the kitchen and not making an effort to pay attention to the diners who are paying their salaries. She gets up to use the restroom and wash her hands. Again, she's disappointed. It's not *"public restroom at a bus station"* dirty, but it's certainly not spotless, and Martha likes her restrooms spotless, especially at a restaurant. Knowing what it takes to start a business, Martha tries to make allowances, but it's getting more difficult to do so the more time she spends at the café.

Returning to her table, the server emerges with Martha's meal and places it on the counter. Martha assumes she needs to pick it up, but just as she stands the server brings it to her. It's a small thing, but she thinks about how nice it would have been if the server had simply said, *"I'll bring your lunch to you as soon as it's ready."* It's another micro-experience that will be added to the file that is automatically being built in Martha's mind.

Let's review. We're always judging. The judgments made are really an evaluation of everything in the environment, asking if it is good for us or bad for us.

Brand is all about emotion. We look at the sum total of our past experiences and future expectations, we factor in what others have told us, and we make a judgment about a product or service. Then we keep evaluating that product or service as we build more experience with it. It's a fluid process, as you can see.

For Martha, it began with the ad that she read. She was influenced by the location of the café and everything she experienced on her drive. Once at the location, the judgments continued as she walked from the parking lot to the front door. More data. More sifting. More judgment.

By the time Martha entered the café, her opinion was already biased. An argument may seem like it's happening inside our head, but it's all really happening in our gut. Our head is justifying why we're feeling the way we are, but our instincts are far ahead of our minds.

As Martha tucks into her lunch, she really enjoys it. The soup tastes fantastic. The vegetables are flavorful and still have life in them. The bread is fresh, and the sandwich ingredients are delicious. There was clearly a huge amount of thought that went into the menu, shopping, and preparation, as simple as it is. And just like that, there's a shift in Martha's experience. Maybe it's worth the less than stellar setting and service for a good lunch. When the bill comes, Martha notices that it's not hers.

Walking back to the counter, she politely tells one of the staff members. The staff member takes the check, disappears into the back without saying a word, and then...nothing. Again, Martha is left in the uncomfortable position of having to call back to the staff. Someone emerges identifying himself as one of the owners and apologizes for the mix up.

He offers Martha a freshly baked brownie to go, on the house, to make up for the mistake. He tells her that they are still working through several issues and again apologizes, asking her to give them another try in a week. He packages the brownie and walks Martha to the door, again thanking her for her business.

As she leaves the café, Martha doesn't quite know what to think. The pros and cons list starts to flow. Weird location. Shorter drive. Great food. Not so good service and less than clean tables. No Wi-Fi. Really honest confession at the end and a lovely gesture to make up for giving her the wrong check.

The fascinating thing is that all of this happens in an instant. A smile or lack thereof. A kind word or a cold attitude. Looking you directly in the eye or staring into the distance. Paying attention to only you or *"multi-tasking."* Every one of these choices that you make when you're interacting with your customers matter.

They are all touchpoints within the touchpoint—additional data points that you are consciously and subconsciously using to test the brand promise. At the heart of everything happening, there is one extraordinarily complex, yet simple, test: how does my experience as a customer compare to the promise of the brand?

And at the core of that test is one word: integrity. You're telling the truth, or you're lying. You have integrity, or you don't.

***

Everything matters. How long you wait and what surrounds you while you wait, including the other patrons, also plays a part in your determination of the brand. That doesn't mean that everyone needs to be all *"scrubbed up."* In fact, how you perceive other people in a public, business environment, e.g. a waiting room, reception area, or grocery store, is determined, in large part, by the environment that the business creates, and not by the individuals who are there with you.

An aside: I'm a huge fan of Trader Joe's, and the store closest to us is actually the happiest place on earth for me. On days when I'm feeling a bit down, I will take my lunch break and go to the store, even if I don't need anything, because the staff makes me feel like a king. I'm recognized and greeted with a smile. They play amazing music throughout the store. Shoppers feel comfortable to sing out loud. Everyone is always smiling.

Yes, they have a wonderful selection of items, wine tastings, and good prices (especially on imported cheeses!), but the real reason I go there is because of the staff and how they make me feel. I've got a big smile plastered on my face as I write this. That's how deeply the experience resonates with me.

The culture at our Trader Joe's is so focused on creating a welcoming and inviting shopping experience that they not only make me feel great, but also alter my perception of everyone else around me. I don't know if those with whom I'm shopping share any of the values that I'm attributing to them, but Trader Joe's created a space in which qualities that I value can flourish.

***

Back at the office, coworkers ask Martha how her lunch was. *"A mixed bag,"* comes her reply. Now Martha's experiences are about to become part of the data files that are being created in the minds of every one of her coworkers.

What will they decide? Will the prospect of a great meal outweigh the other factors? Will they be put off by spotty service and a less than clean space? Will the sincere gestures and honest confession of the owner at the end of the experience sway them?

The answer will be different for everyone, but the point is that their files are now being populated with Martha's retelling of her experience. Keep this in mind as you think about your business. No one's experience exists in a vacuum. The information gets passed along every time.

In the previous chapter, I shared what was arguably a perfect experience at my doctor's office. That does not happen by chance. It was perfectly orchestrated from the first telephone call to the procedure to the follow up phone call. They understood and practiced elite service.

It could have gone differently.

What if I had been escorted into the exam room without any information about what was going to happen next or when the doctor would see me?

How long will the wait be? I hear people pass by outside, but no one sticks their head in to update me on what's happening.

What if the exam room was not a state-of-the-art facility? How would that have made me feel?

What if the doctor had walked in staring at the chart and not immediately greeted me? Would I have been pleased that he's deep in the notes or would I wish he'd look up and acknowledge me?

What if a deep inhale and exhale by the doctor, without saying anything, followed. What effect would that have on me?

As you might imagine, there are almost limitless ways that the scenario could play out, from this less-than-stellar example to the elite care that I actually did receive.

Put yourself in this scenario and continue along.

What if the nurse had checked in every five minutes to let you know how close you were to being seen? Would that have mattered? Or was it enjoyable to have time to sit back in a chair in a quiet room having no interactions? Businesses that are clear about their brand make choices based on what they declare their brand to be. Properly executed, those choices will be reflected in the smallest details, and regardless of whether you would have chosen to make those same choices if you owned the business, the continuity will be apparent.

During the exam, how does the physician conduct herself? Most office visits are scheduled to have the MD in the room for seven minutes of total time, fifteen minutes if it's a first-time visit.

How is that short bit of time being used? Are your questions being answered? Are your questions being anticipated and answered before you can ask them?

Do you feel like you need to have gone to medical school to be able to understand what's being said? What happens if you hear that you need to get a blood test, or an X-ray, or some other diagnostic test? What else do you need to hear to lessen your anxiety? Why are the additional tests necessary? Is the lab on site or do you need to make another appointment, miss another few hours from work, and go to yet another office?

How is check-out handled? Do you speak with anyone about follow up, or are you simply told to call back for your results? Does anyone escort you out, or are you left to find your way on your own? I've had my share of scares, and they always leave me a bit disoriented, particularly when I'm expected to use a different route on the way out.

Finally, how does the staff treat you as you leave? Too often, after the service is rendered, or the product is sold, the promise of the brand seems to disappear. There's a sense that attention has shifted to the new prospect, customer, or in our example, the new patient.

Many medical providers are now combining the traditional office experience with an online component. There are some wonderful advantages to this service, including the convenience of being able to connect with a provider day or night, the ability to make, change, or cancel appointments, the opportunity to see your lab results as soon as they're posted without having to go back to the office, and in some cases, the ability to virtually communicate with your doctor via video.

What could your company offer via an app? I use Marriott Hotels, Delta Air Lines, and Southwest Airlines when I travel. Their apps save them money and make me feel great. I'm in control of my experience, and if I need a person, they're one tap on the app away.

The purpose of doing a deep-dive into these examples is to think of how this applies to your business. You may not be a restaurant owner or medical services provider, but look at each component that we've discussed. They apply across all disciplines.

If you, the business owner, pay no attention to your brand, it will be defined for you in a haphazard fashion, with no consistency. Given that your brand is your promise, not being able to define your brand means that you do not know what you are promising your consumers and what emotions you are hoping to evoke. Everything becomes a roll of the dice.

There's something refreshing about certainty in an uncertain world. Think of any number of businesses that you can count on, be they brick and mortar or online. When you walk in the door, or pull up their website, there's no anxiety. You know what to expect, and as long as you continue to get it, they've made good on their brand promise. If, from time to time, the bar is raised and your experience is enhanced, all the better. It decreases the likelihood that you're going to look elsewhere for the same product or service, even if you find it at a lower price. Why? Because, for most people, there is something wonderful about being able to count on a business to consistently deliver on their promise. *"I know what I'm getting, and I get it every time."* There's just no replacing that sentiment.

We are relationship-oriented creatures, even if the relationship is with a website. There are those of us who may crave excitement in particular areas of our lives, but most of us want to know what to expect when it comes to commerce and to have our expectations met or exceeded.

Again, it is the feeling that counts most here. Do I feel safe? Do I feel like both my personal information and payment information are stored securely? So many pieces of a transaction contribute to this from the look and feel of the page to the user experience in navigating the steps to purchase to the responsiveness of the site.

You can, and should, map this experience yourself for your own business, or for the business you intend to launch. And then the map must be operationalized.

Your ultimate goal is to convert prospects to customers and to make raving fans, advocates, and ambassadors out of every customer.

It will do no good to create a map if you're not going to share it with the entire team. Have it easily accessible online for your staff, and if you're also in an office together, post a hard copy of it in the break room where people can see it. Use it like a war map or some other less-violent example. The point is you want to be leveling up every day, asking where customers had an easy time on the journey and where they stumbled. You'll also want to ask *"Why?"* Not just why they stumbled, but why they succeeded. You can't replicate success unless you understand the reasons why it happened in the first place.

KEY TAKEAWAYS:

- If you don't know where you are, you can't chart a course to where you want to go.

- Map the experience that you want your customers to have.

- There is literally no detail too small.

- If you already have a business, map and compare the experience you want customers to have with the experience they're already having.

- Walk through the completed map, physically or virtually, and look for three things:
  - Where something could fail at each touchpoint, and how you can guard against it
  - Where you could do something more efficiently or effectively.
  - Where you could strategically provide *"Wow"* moments.

- We are, by nature, judgmental, and we are always judging.

- Every experience your customer has with you is evaluated and placed somewhere on one side of the scale or the other. That's why every detail matters.

PUT IT INTO PRACTICE:

- With your team, or initially by yourself, draw out your customer experience map.
- It doesn't have to be perfect. Just get something on paper or on a whiteboard.
- Start with their entry point to your business and proceed from there.
- If your team is not already involved, bring them in and start filling in the details.
- At each touchpoint you should be asking:
  § What could go wrong?
  § Can we create a *"Wow"* moment?
  § How can we enhance the overall experience?
  § Is there a transition, e.g. handoff from one department to another, and if so, how are we ensuring that the transition is smooth?
  § Where are the *"tell a friend"* moments that happen along the way?
  § What emotions do you want to be evoking?
  § Would the current experience that you've described lead a customer to become a brand advocate?

Details matter. This is the kind of focus you'll need as you map your customer's ideal journey. I hope you'll take the time to do this, because it is KEY for your success as a business. In addition to creating a map, this chapter was about creating relationships and creating experiences inside of relationships. It's especially important to have those relationships when something goes wrong.

Chapter Four is about training. It's about taking the good work that you've done and making sure that it becomes real in the lives of your team. Like all of this work, it is virtually useless if you're not sharing what you're doing with everyone in the company. You can't expect people to deliver the promise of your brand if they don't know the experience that they're supposed to create for your customers.

CHAPTER FOUR
TRAIN

Do you love what you do? Is your product or service filling a need? How? Is it unique? Are you providing something that others are also providing, but doing it better, cheaper, faster, or with higher quality? Loving what you do and helping others meet a need brings meaning to work and will make your team trainings far more effective. Why? Because your passion for your work and for others will elevate the experience by instilling the same values in your staff.

Growing up in California's San Joaquin Valley, just about every activity imaginable was within a two-hour drive: skiing (both snow and water), fishing, air shows at Castle Air Force Base, San Francisco, and Yosemite National Park.

We used to rent a trailer and take an extended weekend trip to Yosemite a couple of times a year. My dad, sister, and I loved it. My mom, well, not so much. While we were out exploring and hiking, she was in a cramped trailer trying to perform miracles with a two-burner stove and the fire pit outside, not to mention having to wash everything in a sink the size of a thimble.

Lesson one: one person's vacation can be another person's burden.

One afternoon, we were all out for a hike. I think my mom had threatened mutiny if we didn't all pitch in so she could have a break. As we approached a lookout, we notice a lot of agitated people. The lookout was protected by a single iron rail so it was more of a warning: don't go any farther unless you're up for a thousand foot fall.

A little boy had walked under the rail and was now standing near the edge. His dad was still on the safe side, and was calling little Johnny to come back. Before I knew it, my dad jumped over the rail, scooped the kid up, and brought him back to his father.

It was a blur to me. All I remember was yelling at my dad to get back. I didn't want him to fall over the edge trying to save some other man's son. When my dad returned, I was shaking and yelled at him, asking why he did that.

His response: because the boy needed someone to help him.

Which, upon reflection, made perfect sense. The driving force of my 93-year-old dad's life is helping those in need and making a contributing to others.

This was over forty years ago, but the lesson stuck: whatever work you do, whatever product or service you provide, take it on from the perspective of contribution, of finding a need and filling it. It may not be as dramatic as saving a kid from plunging to his death, but there is satisfaction in knowing that what you're offering is meeting another person's need.

***

In this chapter you'll learn what it takes to move the information you've been given from theoretical to practical. We'll discuss how important it is to be your brand internally because your company is where you incubate, grow, and fine-tune your brand. We'll provide practical exercises to help your team integrate mission, values, and culture, and make sure that there is consistency in every aspect of who *"you"* are as a company.

Keep this in mind as you move through the process: if you can identify what you love about what you do, and the need that you fill, you're going to amplify your all-around success, both in life and in business.

Walk through the map you've created with your team. Ask them what an extraordinary experience looks like, sounds like, and feels like at every touchpoint. Get into the weeds. Let them know what they are empowered to do to deliver that experience. Be specific. The Ritz Carlton provides their staff members a $2,000 allotment per incident to turn around a bad customer experience. If your team members know the parameters within which they can operate without approval to either enhance a good experience or to remedy a bad one, not only will customers be thrilled when they get an unexpected *"Wow"* moment or when their problem is promptly corrected, but your staff will feel more engaged in their work. Why? Because having some degree of autonomy is one of the best predictors of a positive inner work life; one that doesn't require extrinsic motivators. A Harvard study confirms this and many other findings that speak to the power of intrinsic motivation as a predictor of the future financial health of the company (Amabile and Kramer, 2011).

It doesn't matter whether it's money, an upgrade, a certificate for future service, free shipping, or something else. What's important is that your team knows that they can independently take action when it's called for.

Many years ago, I had the pleasure of working with an acting coach who talked about the importance of making sure the stage was stocked with props. Not that we would use them all, but that they would be there as part of our arsenal. The entire focus of her coaching was on being present with your partner on stage, using the available props as needed.

It's the same principle in business. Be present. Listen. Know what's available. If your team is empowered to make certain decisions, such as giving a refund on the spot, you can minimize the *"I'll get back to you"* responses. Customers want three things from you when there is a problem:

1. Own it.
2. Apologize for it.
3. Resolve it in the moment.

While you're at it, provide some sort of token of appreciation for their business and as a further means of demonstrating that you're truly sorry things went wrong.

Begin with the intent. As mentioned several times, if you're not deliberately creating your brand, those who experience it will define it for you. If you're not deliberately training your teams, then the experiences they offer your customers will most likely vary from person to person and may or may not be an accurate reflection of your brand.

Your team must know the customer experience map, with all of its touchpoints. They must know the brand promise which lies at the heart of all you do. They need to understand your company's mission and the values on which it is founded. But it really goes beyond that. Your team must be able to do more than recite your *"core values."* They need to understand how those values inform both their work and how they treat fellow team members and customers.

How you communicate and interact with each other and the cultural attributes of your company come into play here as well.

Your teams also need a deep understanding that brand is a promise that you live, not a motto or slogan that gets plastered on the wall. It has to be delivered with consistency and reflected in every touchpoint a customer has, from your advertising and social media, to your physical space, to your online presence.

CUSTOMER EXPECTATIONS

Keep your word

There are some standard expectations that customers have when approaching any business. New customers have more than likely already researched your business online, read customer reviews, and probably checked with people they trust. Our neighborhood has a private Facebook page. Without fail, multiple times a week, people put out a recommendation call for a plumber, electrician, landscaper, babysitter, etc., and the most common descriptor is *"trust."*

Trust is a fragile thing. It is first established when you keep your promise. A broken promise, not delivering on your word, or having your product or service fall short puts you on an express ride to broken trust. And given that we are wired to look for the negative because of our survival-oriented DNA, even with trust restored, the negative experience remains.

Let your team know that even a *"white lie"* is still a lie, and trust is the casualty.

Personalized experience

Perhaps it's the decreased amount of time we now spend physically interacting with other humans that has led to us wanting more personalized online experiences and more individualized attention when we're directly speaking with someone at a business.

What can your team do to remember clients and also make them feel special when seeing them face to face? What can you do online to reward people, to celebrate a life event like a birthday, or to otherwise let people know that they're more than a number? An email, a thank you call from customer care, a postcard in the mail, all of these things will make a customer pause, if only for a moment, and smile. That's worth a lot.

Anticipate needs

Whether it's an online user experience, talking with someone at customer support, or interacting in person at your store, being told by your customer that the experience was intuitive is one of the best compliments possible.

That means that your customer felt guided through a digital experience. Or they felt that you not only listened, but that you empathized with their situation and were able to anticipate their needs. Maybe you remembered previous challenges and purchases and synthesized the information to provide them a custom solution. It is both an art and a science no matter how it's being delivered, and it's worth taking time to learn it, or in the case of an online user experience, hiring an expert to create it.

On a recent stay at a hotel in Paris, upon checking in I shared with the staff that I was heading to the South of France for a month-long language course the next day. When I returned that evening, there was a pocket-sized French-English dictionary on my nightstand for me to take along with a handwritten note wishing me well. I used it every day and thought of them every time.

Answer questions

People want questions answered quickly, completely, and accurately. Most consumers do research before making a purchase and are primed to buy if they can get all of their questions answered to their satisfaction. *"I don't know..."* followed by abject silence is one of the quickest ways to damage your brand, lose a sale, and possibly receive the gift of a lousy online review and a terrible word of mouth recommendation.

Everyone dealing with customers through any means: phone, chat, email, or in person, must be well-versed in the product or service that they are representing. If they legitimately don't know an answer, they need to know where to go to find it and how long it will take to get the question answered. They need to be able to communicate that to the customer, in real time, and then make good on the promise of the follow-up.

Be kind

A colleague who works at a healthcare company reported that reviewing their call center data led to an interesting discovery. The number one reason that people commended a customer service representative was not for being able to give them everything they wanted, e.g. an appointment with a certain physician on a certain day at a certain time. That was important. But most important was kindness.

"He treated me kindly."

"She listened and understood my situation and was kind to me."

This takes a degree of emotional intelligence, and people that come by it naturally will help your business grow exponentially. Likewise, if you're someone who possesses this gift, know your value!

You can teach the basics, though, for those who do not come by it naturally. Flip the script. In this example, ask the call center staff to recall a time when they were treated kindly by a customer service agent. What did they feel? How did the person speak with them? What did their voice sound like? What was the tempo of the call? What qualities do they remember that still stand out?

Most of the time, that's really all it takes. People need to be guided to remember a time when they experienced something exceptional and then to imitate it. With time and continued coaching, most people will be able to develop the ability to create solutions in those moments.

Solve problems

This cannot be overstated: The power of promise as it relates to your brand is NOT perfection. Rather, it is a guarantee of integrity. I may not get it right every time, but I'll make it right no matter what. That's what people are looking for.

Most everyone knows that perfect doesn't exist. There will always be a time when something doesn't go the way it was intended. Fix it. Solve it. Make it right. And then give them something extra that shows them that they matter as your customer.

To repeat the the age-old formula for confession: Admit you screwed up and say you're sorry. (A real apology by the way is not: *"I'm sorry you feel this way."* A real apology is *"I'm sorry that we did this."*) Then make it right. And finally, go above and beyond to offer something as a means to express both your sorrow over the situation and your appreciation for your customer.

But by all means fix it. And to do that, you have to empower your team to be able to do more than say *"I'll look into it."* To the point at the top of the chapter, they need to know the parameters within which they can operate. Can they offer a gift card for a delayed or lost order, and if so, for what amount? Are they allowed to expedite an order and not charge for shipping? If someone wants an exchange in the store, how can that process be simplified so as not to make the customer feel like they are *"the bad guy"*?

I'm repeating this because the number of times I've come across employees who don't know what they can do to help me is troubling. Even a small problem becomes exaggerated.

I had an experience with a botched Amazon order recently. My first chat with customer service and the subsequent call left me feeling that the situation would quickly be resolved.

The rep apologized for the errors made in not getting the printer out to me when promised, sent me an email confirming that it would be shipped the next day to my location, and extended my Amazon Prime membership with a very sincere apology for the inconvenience that they had caused.

So far, so good. It's also worth noting that when I was on the phone with the rep, there was no sense that she was reading from a script. The conversation was natural, and she seemed genuinely interested in helping me by getting the printer to me as soon as possible.

The next day came and went, with no printer arriving. I called again that evening. The same promise was made, another email was sent. The next day, I called mid-day to make sure the delivery would happen, and was again assured that it would. End of day came and went, and again, no printer. I called back that evening and was *again* promised that delivery would happen the next day.

By this time, a few key points became obvious: the team at customer service was truly empowered. They offered extensions on membership, they had the ability to communicate with the local station and determine the location of the package, and they felt confident enough to make promises that I could only assume they thought would be kept.

They were also trained in, or came equipped with, the skill set essential for good communication: being able to listen and to respond. It seems so simple, but it's really not. More on this ahead.

So what began as a sincere attempt to make things right became a seemingly endless loop of promises that had less and less impact as time went on. I expressed, as politely as possible, that after hearing the assurance the second, third, and finally the fourth time, each promise seemed a bit emptier.

By the end, they had extended my Prime membership for a year—which was appreciated—but I had to spend a couple of days using our local FedEx Office for my printing needs. First world problems, without a doubt, but as a growing business, everything matters.

When the package finally arrived, my feeling for Amazon was not what it was a week earlier. I'll still use them. In many ways, they're the only game in town, but the warm and fuzzy *"isn't this relationship the best?!?"* feeling that I once had was gone. It will more than likely return, but the fact that I'm recounting this now should tell you something. Bad experiences, particularly after so many positive ones, stick with customers.

I liken it to a relationship where everything is going so well, there's not even a thought that something at some time might go wrong. My defenses were down. Amazon said it would be here in two days, shipped free, because of my Prime membership. All of my previous experiences told me that the printer would be delivered on time, or early.

In this case, I don't know what else could have been done. The final rep that I dealt with shared with me that the package was improperly sorted multiple times before finally escaping the station and making it to the truck. But the reason didn't matter. For me, it was a perfect illustration of brand evoking emotion, reminiscent of the emotions evoked by personal relationships.

The bottom line is that things will go wrong. You will miss getting an order out on time. A customer will feel that one of your staff members treated them rudely. Recall the statistic mentioned earlier in this book–that globally, one third of all customers will leave a brand they love after one bad experience.

Do everything that you can to minimize those bad experiences, and everything that you can to make it right when they do happen.

BASELINE, UNDERSTANDING WHERE YOU ARE, AND MOVING FORWARD

Here's a method that I've found useful when working with clients. As with everything, you can execute this on your own or hire a professional to lead the process.

Beginning with on-site observation, take an objective look at your physical site(s) and employee interactions with customers and with each other, at retail outlets, corporate offices, call centers, fulfillment centers, and other key locations.

Conduct confidential interviews with employees, customers, board members, and shareholders with the goal of identifying gaps and inconsistencies in knowledge and delivery of services. Review customer feedback data from whatever sources you're using to gather it or create a feedback mechanism. Look for trends and surface quick-fixes that can be implemented immediately. It's always nice to have some wins straight out of the gate.

CUSTOMER EXPERIENCE AND
CUSTOMER JOURNEY

We talked above about creating the desired map of your customer's experiences, which is a key part of the work that we do with clients. After reviewing the customer feedback data, compare their actual experience to the mapped experience that you would like them to have. Look for the places that customers are leaving and also rejoining the journey and why that may be happening.

Based on those results, you'll be well positioned to design the kinds of experiences that people will want to have repeatedly. Remember that no matter what your company does, everyone is in the hospitality business, and your customer should be treated as a guest. Everyone on your team, regardless of job description, has a role in delivering the promise of your brand.

Using your mission, values, and culture along with the promise of your brand, position yourself to your target audiences, refine your messages, and state your value proposition in a compelling way. If possible, personify your brand, and find the voice that fits it and the emotions that you want to evoke in your prospects, customers, and employees.

The final step is to create an executable, customer service strategy. As with all of this work, it must be shared with everyone so that everyone can own it. Teams function at their highest when everyone is individually owning responsibility and working together.

In training your team, here are some additional recommendations to consider:

Review your Mission, Values, and Brand.
 — Ask: are we fulfilling on who we say we are?

- If so, great.
- If not, correct your course.

Set up your team for success.
- Train them well.
- Have ongoing training that addresses changes in policies and procedures.
- Let them know that they can share process breakdowns with you without fear.
- Work with them to correct those breakdowns.
- Monitor them as a means of supporting them.

Promise only what you know you can deliver every time.
- It is better to consistently deliver on what you promise than to overpromise and only deliver on some items.

Look for ways to raise the bar on a regular basis.
- Recognize that what may have become routine for you can potentially be an extraordinary life experience for your customers, and treat them accordingly.
- Conflict with a customer is not an opportunity to prove that you're right and she or he is wrong; it's an opportunity to produce a breakthrough from a breakdown.

Language matters.
- I'm sorry if you misunderstood me / No, that's not what I said.
  VS.
- **I'm sorry if I wasn't clear in my explanation.**

NOTE: Again, you're not here to prove anything. Give up the need to be right.

- Speaking to another staff member (in front of, or not in front of, the customer) *"He said he has a frequent purchaser account, but it is not here."*
  VS.
- "The gentleman / The lady / Mr. Jones / Mrs. Jones / Steve / Jane (whatever is appropriate) has a frequent purchaser account, but I am not able to find it. Would you please help me find it?"

Note: There is a HUGE difference between using the word *"said"* and simply stating the concern as a fact. *"Said"* sets up a he said-she said dynamic and implies that someone is not telling the truth.

- I don't know why Sam told you that. It's wrong.
  VS.
- Let me check with Sam and find out why you were told that. In the meantime, it will be my pleasure to take care of whatever you need.
- Avoid "no problem." And use "you're welcome", "my pleasure", or "I'm glad I could be of help."

Emotional response matters.

- Meet people where they are at in order to take them to where you want them to be. NOTE: this doesn't mean to meet anger with anger. It simply means to acknowledge what someone is feeling at the time as calmly as possible.

Greet customers by name, if you know them.
- If not, use polite terms that are organic to you, e.g. the gentleman, the lady, folks, fellas.

Work as a team—you rise and fall together.
- Establish seamless transitions.
- Establish a fail-safe means of communicating.
- Get sufficient input before instituting any changes in policy or procedures.
- Do a *"soft launch"* of the changes.
- Announce the launch date internally.
- Walk through every possible breakdown that can occur and the solutions for each one.
- Adjust for those breakdowns to minimize the chances of them happening.

Customer Experience tends to be a reflection of how the entire staff treats one another, and how their superiors treat them.
- Model the way you want your customers to be treated.
- Review complaints that you receive.
- Deal with them promptly and effectively.
- Look internally to see where this same problem may be happening.

Hospitality at every turn
- *"Good morning," "good afternoon," "it's good to see you," "thank you," "please, follow me,"* and *"let me show you to your table"* should all be standard vocabulary, and *you* should take the lead.

***

Your company is where your brand is incubated and fine-tuned. If you can't be true to your brand with your team, you'll never be as successful when delivering it to your customers.

Be transparent with your teams. Establish solid relationships and help your team members gain fluency in leadership and communication skills, and in dealing with upset and resolving conflicts. (All of these topics are covered in Chapter 5.) By doing so, you'll give your teams the solid foundation they need to effectively interact with your customers.

Make sure they understand that your brand is your promise to your customers. Help them get clear on what it ideally looks like, sounds like, and feels like to have your brand come alive in the experience of your customers.

Let your staff know that although you own your brand, once you launch it into the wild, it lives in the emotional experience of your customers. If they're not experiencing it as you intended, you have some work to do. The only way to know if it is, is to ask. That's why customer surveys are invaluable tools.

Challenge your teams to show up at work being brand ambassadors. Why does this matter? For two reasons. First, because you start each day fully engaged, without any need to *"warm up."* Second, because if your team lives up to the term, it will naturally inspire your customers to become brand ambassadors as well.

How do you make training your team something more than lectures and checklists? Take flight at 30,000 feet and engage them in brainstorming. Enjoy the view with them by sharing your vision and your passion. Look up and out and around. Take a deep breath, and think of what could be.

Let them know that you value their input, and that the process is safe. Brainstorming is just that: a storm. It can be messy, exciting, unpredictable, and sometimes frightening, but it's always a great way of connecting everyone to each other, as long as there is trust.

This was demonstrated by the recently concluded *"Project Aristotle,"* where Google researched what makes teams successful. After interviewing hundreds of team members along with team leads and executives, they concluded that even more important than which individuals were on each team was the concept of psychological safety. Team members trusted one another.

Google stated that, *"In a team with high psychological safety, teammates feel safe to take risks around their team members. They feel confident that no one on the team will embarrass or punish anyone else for admitting a mistake, asking a question, or offering a new idea (Dubey, 2016)."*

Brainstorming in a safe space is a great way to identify emerging leaders. Emerging leaders rise up when they know their opinion is valued, and when they are encouraged to take the time to delve into important factors that affect your business. They'll find themselves contributing in ways they never previously imagined. They'll think creatively. They'll take risks. When they fail, you can teach the principle of *"fail fast, fail often, fail forward."*

Team members, regardless of position, who regularly apply and engage the vision and the passion that you share, are able to bring their growing knowledge base into 360-degree conversations with their fellow team members, managers, directors, and the C-Suite.

Solving problems, especially in larger companies, can often forgo involving front-line and lower-level staff. Don't miss out on the treasure trove of wisdom that is more than likely residing in all of your staff members. This is your opportunity to encourage everyone to claim a stake in the future of your brand, and to contribute to it.

Reward those who do rise up. Give them the tools they need for their ongoing growth and development. Encourage them to continue to reach, to gain perspective, to expand their knowledge, to get distinctly different views on a situation in order to see it clearly, and to take calculated risks.

Create a standardized system to capture, consider, and, if appropriate, implement ideas. If you do institute something that one of your staff members recommended, let everyone know. There's nothing quite as satisfying as acknowledgement.

By sharing your vision and your inspiration, and inviting everyone around you to join in, you communicate that you trust them, which is one of the greatest gifts that you can give. The vast majority of people want to demonstrate that they are worthy of the trust that is placed in them.

This will also help you stay focused on the highest and best use of your time. Finally, as you do the work of raising up leaders from among the ranks, you're giving them the skills to do the same for those whom they manage.

✳✳✳

Walking through Oakland Airport many years ago, an Instagram-worthy toddler opened up his arms and started wobbling towards me. He had a grin from ear to ear, which brought such joy to my heart. I stopped and stooped over exclaiming, *"Hey buddy!"* His mom scooped him up, and as she was walking away, I heard her say, *"He's diseased, you have to stay away from him!"*

It was about three years into what ended up being a seven-year journey with a disease called Vitiligo. It's an autoimmune disorder which affects one percent of the total population world-wide, and I had it. Vitiligo is characterized by the absence of pigment on certain areas of your body. It is in no way contagious, and it's still a mystery as to why I have it even though I have the best doctor on the planet for this disease, as you'll read below.

In my case, I lost all the pigment on my face. My ethnic background is Armenian, Assyrian, Greek, and Italian, and my natural pigmentation is very dark, so losing all the pigment on my face made me stand out in a crowd.

I loved going out at night, particularly to dark restaurants or clubs, where people really couldn't see the difference. But during the daylight, there was no escaping it. I had launched my consulting business just before the onset of this disease, and every morning I had to give myself the mother of all pep-talks to get out of bed, get dressed, and venture out into the world.

On some level, you get used to the stares, the subtle and not so subtle movements of people moving away from you as you navigate a crowd. You get used to strangers asking if you have *"Michael Jackson's disease,"* and you begin to think of it as an opportunity to educate others about the disease even though you'd like to tell them to do something else with their questions.

But on some level, you never get used to being seen as a leper. And that's really how it felt. I packed on thirty-plus pounds. My self-esteem was in the toilet. But I got up every day and kept at it.

I thought about suicide. It's weird to write this for the first time because it feels like a lifetime away. I was fortunate to have a loving husband, wonderful family and friends, and supportive church communities who sustained me through this. And I was fortunate to find the world's premier dermatologist dealing with Vitiligo in Los Angeles, where I lived. When I walked into her office for the first time, she said, *"We're going to get all your pigment back."* No hesitation. That's how it's going to be. She knew her brand. Healing.

Something clicked inside me. If there's hope, then I want to be ready for it. I took on a twelve-week nutrition and exercise program, posted a calendar on the fridge, and X'd off each day after attending the gym and sticking to my eating program.

I stuck Post-it notes on the bathroom mirror with inspirational messages, gave thanks to God for my healing before it occurred, and *"saw"* myself with my pigment fully restored.

Three months later, the weight I had gained was gone, and I was in fighting shape. Spots of pigment were appearing on my face thanks to a new topical medication that was in its trial phase, and, I believe, thanks to my visualization and prayer. And within a year, it was as if the disease had never touched me.

From time to time it reoccurs, and my physician is there, walking the journey with me again, with the same commitment she had on day one. *"We're going to get this back."*

From the outset of that seven-year journey, I decided something and I carried it into my consulting work: treat every human being I meet with compassion, and go out of my way to befriend those who are different, who are outcasts, who are alone.

I resolved to help my clients recognize that their customers are more than numbers, that they are people. By acting with integrity and treating every prospect and customer with respect and dignity, while at the same time delivering on the promise of their brand, they would do more to attract and retain customers than any marketing ploy could give them.

Compassion is my personal brand. What's yours? Because as you move from job to job, or company to company, there is only one thing that goes with you: yourself. You bring your personal brand into everything that you do whether at home, at work, or on the road.

It's a good idea to encourage your team to think about their personal brand as well. How do they want people to know them? What's their promise to the world? Just as it is for your company and mine, if they don't decide for themselves, the world will decide for them.

KEY TAKEAWAYS:

- Your company is where you incubate, grow, and fine-tune your brand. Therefore, model how you want your customers to be treated within your team.
- Start at the beginning—you need to know that your team understands what an extraordinary customer experience looks like, sounds like, and feels like at every touchpoint of your map. If they don't, you need to show them.
- Encourage emerging leaders by giving them the tools they need to grow.

- Experiences that feel personalized, even if many people are receiving them, are good things.

- Encourage team members to think about and share their personal brand. It will pay huge dividends in terms of customer experience.

- Language matters! Give your team guidelines, such as a standards by which customers are addressed.

Let your team know that they are empowered to solve problems and provide *"wow"* moments for customers. Give them specific parameters, so they can act quickly and without concern.

PUT IT INTO PRACTICE:

– Get real with your team. How well do each of you represent your brand internally?

– Depending on the answer, create a plan to address the areas of need, a timeline to accompany it, and the deliverables. Agree on someone to oversee it.

– Rate yourself and your team on the following:

§ Keeping your word – relentlessly.

§ Personalizing experiences for your customers.

§ Anticipating customer needs.

§ Answering questions quickly, completely, and accurately.

§ Being kind and using appropriate language.

§ Solving problems.

– How well-equipped does your team feel to deliver the promise of your brand to your customers?

Depending on the answers, create a plan to address the areas of need, a timeline to accompany it, and the deliverables. Assign someone to be responsible for it.

In this chapter, we learned how to train your staff, and to make sure that your team knows what it should feel like, look like, and sound like to deliver an extraordinary customer experience. Because brand is emotional, your team learned strategies for evoking the emotions that you want your customers to feel. They also learned that the brand must be consistently delivered in every aspect of a customer's experience.

In the final chapter, we'll learn what it means to deliver your brand. In essence, what it means to be your brand by living it out. We'll take the training from the chapter you've just finished out of the dugout and onto the field. (In my mind, it's always baseball season.) We'll learn about leadership, communication, dealing with upset, and conflict resolution.

This book is premised on not only delivering the promise of your company's brand by being your word, but by being your word in every aspect of your life: at work and at home, with your team, your family, and your friends.

CHAPTER FIVE
DELIVER

Delivering the promise of your brand through great customer experiences means developing fluency in leadership, communication, dealing with upset, and conflict resolution. Hundreds, if not thousands, of books have been written about these topic areas and subsets within them. No book, however, can cover every possible scenario. Challenge yourself to develop an elite level of knowledge in each area and then practice drawing from your knowledge base to navigate each unique situation that arises.

***

In speaking with a client about developing an app for use in the healthcare field, he realized that his lead engineer, who was extraordinary at development, lacked the leadership skills necessary to scale the company and the product. He also lacked the technical expertise required to make sure that the app was compliant with regulatory issues.

He and his partner knew that they wanted the engineer to stay with the company. They wanted him to continue to bring his considerable skill set to product development and user experience, but it became clear after two years that he was not the person to lead the team into this next critical phase of growth.

They did not anticipate any problems. He owned options in the company. He was well paid. He would continue to do what he did really well and wouldn't have the pressure of trying to come up to speed on scalability or regulatory matters.

Outages had already occurred as a result of his inability to forecast usage and scale up, and there were significant prospects on the horizon, which would demand a level of technical knowledge about regulations that neither the owners nor the lead engineer possessed.

The owners had offered the engineer every opportunity to gain the skills necessary, including bringing in a top-notch CFO to coach him in order to lead the team and ensure that the requirements were met. His response: *"I'm good."*

They had what they thought would be a very easy conversation with him. They were going to hire another engineer with the skill set that they needed to lead the project. He would continue in his current position, but would report to the new hire.

There was visible upset when the news was shared, and the engineer gave them an ultimatum. If the new hire was to lead the team, then he would quit. This was a big deal to the owners. They knew this man personally. They went to the same church together. Their kids played together. Their wives spent time together.

More distressing was the fact that it would take months to find someone capable of coming up to speed on the work that had been done to build the app if he did leave, meaning they would not hit their benchmarks for the quarter.

So, in order to *"smooth over"* the upset, they gave the engineer a raise. It had been two years without one and he deserved it, but the timing and the reason were all wrong. What they ended up communicating was that if you get upset and threaten to leave, you get a raise.

They also communicated, without knowing it, that he was still the team lead because the next day he felt empowered to recommend three new hires, which they had to delay. They considered a compromise: keep the current engineer on and hope to hit the benchmarks, and then tell him that they had a new hire who would become the team lead. It would *"only"* be a month and a half. What could possibly go wrong in six weeks?

A deeper dive into this situation revealed that the story playing on an endless loop in the minds of the company's owners was one of disaster. From their perspective, the engineer would never stay on if he could not be the project lead. He'd give two weeks' notice—hopefully—and then leave, and they'd be unable to hit their benchmarks. They would lose current clients and be unable to obtain new clients. This story was informing all of their thinking and decision making.

I asked one simple question: from a place of integrity, what's the solution? They answered: to let him know now.

Here's the coaching that followed:

You KNOW that this is the right decision. It's the right decision for the owners, for the company, for the team, and for the clients that you serve. Taking a gamble with regulatory requirements and people's medical records is inexcusable.

It's the right decision for the engineer. He gets to continue to code, which is what he loves, and, if he decides to stay, he has the opportunity to learn by observation those skills he lacks, and take these skills with him if and when he does choose to leave.

Knowing that it's the right decision in your head is worthless unless you also feel it in your heart.

Determine no more than three key points that you want to convey. People cannot retain more information than that.

Practice the delivery of the message aloud. Things sound different in your mind than they do coming out of your mouth. Practice with your business partner. Practice alone in front of the mirror.

This is not a negotiation. This is a fait accompli. A done deal. Let him know that this is the best decision for the company, the team, and the customers whom you serve, and that you want him to continue to be a part of the company as you grow.

People respect leaders. People respect having structure. The engineer may very well respond far more positively to you showing up with a spine attached than he did when he knew he could steamroll you for a raise.

Tell a different story. Tell the story that ends with *"yes."*

Walk into the meeting with the courage of your convictions. Your job is not to predict what might happen, but to be present, deliver the news powerfully and with respect, and make the invitation.

You'll deal with his answer after he gives it. Whatever his answer is, it's just input, and it will inform your next move. Because at this point, it's all speculation.

There are a ton of lessons packed into this story. As you will read in this final chapter, leadership, communication, dealing with upset, and conflict resolution not only apply to how you approach your customers, but also how you approach internal issues.

***

This is where the rubber meets the road. When you move from theoretical to practical, you're going to have breakdowns. That's how you learn and grow. So embrace the breakdowns. They can be transformed into breakthroughs. Besides, it's just input, remember?

If you learn, practice, and master the skills of leadership, communication, dealing with upset, and conflict resolution, you'll be well-equipped to handle anything that comes your way.

All of these skills will help you not only be the promise of your brand, but in doing so retain your customers. It is easier and cheaper to retain current customers than it is to get them back, and certainly much easier and cheaper than getting new ones.

Remember this when you're asking if it's worth the *"trouble"* to resolve customer conflicts and manage upset toward a mutually satisfying resolution.

In my annual report of my past year of flying, Delta Air Lines let me know that I'm in the top 4% of all frequent flyers. My loyalty, as evidenced by my status, is of great value to them. I went from a one-time customer in 2001 to a brand advocate.

I'm invested in this airline. I've built up a storehouse of goodwill for them, which makes me more forgiving of the occasional less-than-stellar experiences. But it also means that the stakes are much higher if I were to be treated in a way that felt like my business no longer mattered. You might say, *"The higher they are, the harder they fall."*

I will add one other point for your consideration. You never know which *"average"* customer will turn into one of your most valued customers, whether they increase the frequency of their buying, or the amount they are spending, or simply by becoming a regular customer, year after year. And you have a significant part to play in moving them in that direction.

You're in a relationship, for better or worse, with all of your customers, and one meaningful act of kindness can work wonders for any relationship. In the introduction, I shared that my spouse covered my mom's casket with 33 gardenias—an unexpected and meaningful act of kindness. What unexpected act of kindness can you do for your customers today?

Since the goal is to create raving fans and brand advocates, no customer should be taken for granted.

You'll notice that much of this chapter is written in bullet point lists. I decided on this format for one reason: practicality. When you have to reach out to an upset customer, or if you're trying to put into practice some important aspects of leadership, a checklist is always easier to reference than a narrative.

You'll also notice that there is overlap from list to list. This is because each topic in some way leans on the others. You can't lead without communicating. You can't communicate without having a conflict from time to time, and so on.

LEADERSHIP

It can sound like nothing more than a buzzword, but becoming a true leader is a lifelong journey. There is nothing simple about it, and it requires daily reflecting and refining. It demands a level of self-awareness and self-confidence that allows you to admit when you are wrong and correct course, and conversely, to hold fast to what is right.

I think of the words of St. Francis de Sales who said, *"Nothing is so strong as gentleness, nothing so gentle as real strength."* He also counseled that we should *"not wish to be anything but who we are, and try to be that perfectly."* Follow these two maxims, and you're well on your way to becoming a great leader.

1. Have integrity. Without this, you are nothing.

2. Adopt an *"I am 100% responsible"* attitude.
   a. Walk into the office each day with the mindset of an owner.
   b. This doesn't mean that you do everything, it just means that whatever your position in the organization, you look at it from an owner's mindset and have the courage to call things out that need to be addressed.

3. Have a vision and hold that 30,000-foot view. Vision inspires, calls, and invites.
   a. Inspire others to become involved by sharing your vision.
   b. Motivate others when necessary. Motivation provides the urgent push when needed from time to time
   c. Create a strategy to fulfill your vision.

4. Build consensus. This means knowing what everyone brings to the table.

5. Learn from your mistakes. More importantly, admit them, and use them as teachable moments for yourself and for those whom you lead.

6. Be calm, cool, and collected. It's a cliché for a reason.

7. Gather the facts from sources you trust, and then act quickly and decisively.
   a. Repeated quick and decisive action helps to overcome fear.

8. Leading as part of a team means you can disagree until the decision is made. Then everyone is united behind the decision.

9. Be humble.
   a. Don't be fake humble, e.g. *"Oh, you're far too kind. I didn't really do anything."* Be real. Say *"thank you."* Take your bows. Acknowledge your team.

10. Acknowledge others relentlessly.

11. Demonstrate persistence.

12. Resolve conflict. Understand why it happened. Reduce future occurrences.

13. Be an astute observer of those who work for you.
    a. Enhance their strengths.
    b. Help them to grow in areas where they are weak.

COMMUNICATION

What passes for communication in most interactions is anything but. The level of distraction that we allow into our lives makes real communication a huge challenge.

Real communication is dialogue that engages two or more people who are willing to be related to one another. It requires that people tell the truth and that they openly share their feelings. It means being vulnerable and being OK with not having the answer before entering the conversation. It means listening, absorbing, processing, and then responding, not just waiting for a comma or period to jump in.

We say what we mean and we mean what we say.

1. Commit to eliminating gossip. Gossip is complaining to someone about a problem that they have no power to solve.
   a. If you have a concern with someone, talk to him or her directly.
   b. If there is a history of mistrust between you, let the other person know you'd like an unbiased third party at the conversation.

2. Actually listen to someone each day. It's an active process.
   a. Voice is most always better than email. Make sure there's enough time for both parties to have their say.
   b. Hear what was said by pausing before you speak after the other person is complete. It helps to shut down the voices in your head.

    c. Ask for clarification if there is something you
don't understand.

    d. Refer back to Tip 1: We mean what we say and we
say what we mean, e.g. *"Did you complete the report?"*
does not actually mean *"I can never trust you to finish
anything on time."*

3. Listen with the possibility of being moved from your
position. It is possible that someone else's point of
view might be a contribution to you.

4. You can acknowledge someone's point of view without
agreeing with her or him. A simple *"got it"* or *"I hear
you"* will suffice.

5. The best time to deal with a disagreement is NOW.
However, do take time to calm down first, if you
need to.

    a. Do not assume it will be better next time. It won't,
because you will add your upset from the first incident
to every succeeding one.

6. Say what is so and only what is so.

    a. Don't sweeten it up.

    b. Don't use anger.

7. Speak from your point of view, and not as a victim. *"I
feel"* not *"you make me feel"* is the way to go.

8. Realize that working as a team means compromise.
Compromise means everyone has to give something
up. And that's OK. Recognizing the feeling of discom-

fort between how things are and how you want things to be is how we grow.

DEALING WITH UPSET

"Embrace the suck." So goes the statement often used in the military. The situation may be tough, but you must deal with it. And the sooner you deal with it, the better, regardless of how *"sucky"* it seems at the time. It will only get worse.

There are always lessons to be learned in dealing with upset. You may learn where you can grow in terms of your leadership or communication skills. You may learn where your processes need revising. You may learn how deeply you have to dig to find the strength to get through, and that if you dig deeply enough, you'll always find the strength. This list is written assuming the upset is coming from the customer. You can easily adapt it to other situations.

1. Begin with the assumption that the problem is real, and that the customer has a right to their feelings, even if that feeling is anger.

2. Do not match their language, intonation, or emotions; listen from a place of concern, but not attachment.

3. Convey your commitment to finding a solution.

4. Allow whatever time is necessary for the customer to get everything said.

5. Tell the customer that you appreciate them bringing the problem to you so you can find the solution.

Paraphrase the important points back to them so they know you listened, and so that you can make sure you heard the essential information in the midst of the upset.

6. Solve it. Immediately, if at all possible. If you can't solve it on your own, be honest and commit to getting back to them within a specific time frame, but regardless, own the problem and don't explain how hard you're going to have to work to make it right. No one cares. They just want their problem solved.

7. Make sure you make it right.

8. After the problem is resolved, have a conversation about it so you can figure out what went wrong, fix the core of the problem, and then share the problem and the solution with the entire team. Then memorialize it.

9. If possible, thank the person who raised the problem in the first place, letting them know that they helped you create a solution. This is a great time to include a token of appreciation, e.g. a gift card, an extension of their subscription, etc.

CONFLICT RESOLUTION

In many ways, resolving conflicts is about mastering both empathy and detachment. You have to remain engaged, but not so deeply that the situation triggers you. This list is written assuming a conflict between staff members but can be adapted to a variety of situations. Sincerity in your desire to reach resolution will carry the day.

Come from a place of co-creation. Both parties should be involved in the problem-solving process. Continue to remind yourself that in making the journey to a solution, the lessons learned along the way are well worth the time invested.

Finally, regardless of the content of the conflict, if you stay focused on the process, you'll be well served. Many times, interpersonal conflict involves *"juicy details"* that distract from the desired end result of resolution. Two questions to keep asking are:

- What are the objective facts of the conflict?
- What is the subjective story that I'm adding to those facts?
- Why do we create a story to go with the facts? Usually to persuade those listening that we're in the right.

1. Be open to hearing from one another when there is a conflict. Your goal is early intervention. Begin with the assumption that the problem is real, and that the other person has a right to their feelings.

2. Do not match their language, intonation, or emotions; listen from a place of concern, but not attachment.

3. Convey your commitment to finding a solution.

4. Allow whatever time is necessary for the other person to get everything said.

5. Tell the other person that you appreciate them bringing the problem to you so you can find the solution together. Paraphrase the important points back to them so they know you listened and so you can make

sure that you heard the essential information in the midst of the upset.

6. Share how you're feeling: *"Here's how it occurred for me"* or *"it landed this way for me."* Note that the language is about how things show up for you with no attempt to discredit the other person's experience.

7. If the upset stems from something substantial, such as a breakdown in process, work together to create a desired end result. Then break the result down into manageable chunks, with a timeline to implement change. This may include regular check-in time with each other.

8. After the problem is resolved, have a conversation about it so you can figure out not only what went wrong, but also how to fix the core of the problem, and then share the problem and the solution with the entire team. Then memorialize it.

KEY TAKEAWAYS:

- You are in a relationship with your team and with your customers.

- Leadership, communication, dealing with upset, and conflict resolution are the skills you and your team will need to work on mastering.

- Help your team develop the mindset of an owner by adopting an attitude of 100% responsibility.

- Remember to look up! A checklist-only mentality will never move you beyond daily tasks, and will destroy creativity, so take your team with you to 30,000 feet on a regular basis.

- Say what you mean and mean what you say.

- Listen with the possibility of being moved from your position.

- When dealing with upset, begin with the commitment to finding a solution.

PUT IT INTO PRACTICE:

- Gather your team and review four key areas necessary to providing an extraordinary customer experience:
  - Leadership
  - Communication
  - Dealing with upset
  - Conflict resolution

- From the above discussion, what areas need improvement?

- What can you do to make sure that your team develops fluency in those areas?

- Create a timeline with deliverables and a person responsible for follow through.

- Are you encouraging your team to take on their individual jobs from a place of 100% responsibility and to have the mindset of an owner? If not, discuss with them what that means to you.

CONCLUSION

"The supreme quality for leadership is unquestionably integrity. Without it, no real success is possible, no matter whether it is on a section gang, a football field, in an army, or in an office."

—General Dwight D. Eisenhower
Supreme Allied Commander in Europe 1943–1945
34th President of the United States of America

***

This book began with a story about my mom and her personal brand—extraordinary hospitality. She was a person of integrity. You could count on her to deliver the promise of her brand in all circumstances, to all people, in all places.

Real success comes when you show up committed to telling the truth, whether at home with your family, enjoying a night out with your friends, or at work with your colleagues. At that point, you have unlimited access to power, because there are no contradictions in your life. No made-up stories to remember. Your word is impeccable.

With customers, if you tell the truth about your brand and deliver your brand promise every time, your customers will return, purchase more, and tell others about you. They'll become raving fans and advocates.

Engage these customers and they can become a team of trusted advisors, telling you the truth about your brand—the good, the bad, and everything in between—from their unique perspective as consumers.

With friends, if you tell the truth with kindness and respect, you'll attract people who also value integrity.

With family, if you tell the truth with love and compassion, you'll elevate yourself as a mom, a dad, a sister or brother, a son or a daughter.

Taken seriously, this work has the potential to be life-changing. If you're living a compartmentalized life, showing up being a different person in different circumstances, and if your relationship to the truth is situational, then integrity isn't truly present. You're acting. You may be doing a good job of acting and still delivering a good product or service, but integrity doesn't exist in some areas of your life and not in others. Integrity is an all or nothing proposition.

So—what is your personal brand?

What is your promise to your friends and family? To the people in your life who support you, love you, engage you, challenge you, and cheer for you. What promise are you willing to make to them, and then keep?

Recall how I dealt with Vitiligo in the story I shared in Chapter Four. My personal brand became compassion. The thing that I lacked and craved was the thing that I gave away in abundance. And in so doing, I ended up receiving much more.

Ask yourself, right now, what promise you are willing to make today. Are you willing to hold yourself to keeping your promise even when no one is checking on you? Are you willing to hold yourself accountable even when no one is looking? Are you willing to do so daily without fail and without compromise, in all places and with all people?

You are the very foundation of this work. Your ability to deliver the promise of your brand to your customers depends on your ability to live your life with integrity and to be in alignment with your personal brand in every aspect of who you are. Start today.

"After enlightenment comes the dishes." It's time to go to work.

WORKS CITED

— Simon Sinek: *Start with Why: How Great Leaders Inspire Everyone to Take Action*, 2009
— David Clarke and Ron Kinghorn: *Experience is everything: here's how to get it right*, 2018
— Amy Gallo: *Harvard Business Review, The Value of Keeping the Right Customers*, 2014
— American Express and Ebiquity: *American Express Customer Service Barometer*, 2017
— Seth Godin: *Seth's Blog, Define: Brand*, 2009
— Teresa Amabile and Steven Kramer, *Harvard Business Review Press: The progress principle: Using small wins to ignite joy, engagement, and creativity at work*, 2011
— Abeer Dubey, et.al: *Project Aristotle by Google*, 2016
— Peter Baumann, co-author of the 2011 book *Ego: The Fall of the Twin Towers and the Rise of an Enlightened Humanity*, whose writing has influenced my thinking for more than two decades.

ACKNOWLEDGMENTS

To the team at Self Publishing School, for their support and encouragement, and for their commitment to helping others succeed.

To my editors, Rachel McCracken and Qat Wanders, for their expert guidance that exceeded expectations.

To my launch team, for helping me soar.

Thank you all.

ABOUT THE AUTHOR

The founder of Mosesian Strategies, Ken Mosesian is passionately committed to connecting businesses to the promise of their brand and helping them keep their promise by delivering extraordinary experiences to their customers. Ken holds a B.A. in Psychology from California State University, Stanislaus

His 20 years of experience leading companies through start-up, growth and turnaround, has helped Ken transform a diverse array of businesses, including law firms, medical and dental practices, health and fitness companies, restaurants, and non-profit organizations. Ken's work focuses on brand and customer experience, strategic planning, communication, and leadership training.

Logging nearly 2,000,000 miles in the air has sharpened Ken's awareness of the disconnect that often exists between what a brand says and what it delivers. These real-world experiences with myriad service providers inform Ken's work, helping him to deliver practical solutions to his clients.

Ken has held corporate marketing positions and worked as the Executive Director and the Development Director of national non-profit organizations. He has served as a Director on several non-profit boards and is an accomplished speaker. Ken has a deep knowledge of LGBTQ issues and is recognized for building trusted partnerships with key stakeholders across all levels.

Made in the USA
Middletown, DE
05 April 2019